AT MY TABLE
Fay Lewis

PHOTOGRAPHY BY NEIL CORDER

Décor styling by Tina Bester
Food styling by Justine Kiggen

This edition published in 2008 in softcover by Struik Publishers
First published in 2005 in hardcover by Struik Publishers
(a division of New Holland Publishing (South Africa) (Pty) Ltd)
New Holland Publishing is a memeber of Avusa Ltd
Cape Town | London | Sydney | Auckland

www.struik.co.za

Cornelis Struik House, 80 McKenzie Street, Cape Town 8001, South Africa
Garfield House, 86–88 Edgware Road, London W2 2EA, United Kingdom
Unit 1, 66 Gibbes Street, Chatswood, NSW 2067, Australia
218 Lake Road, Northcote, Auckland, New Zealand

10 9 8 7 6 5 4 3 2 1

Publishing manager: Linda de Villiers
Editor: Joy Clack
Designer (content pages): petaldesign
Designer (cover): Helen Henn
Photographer (content pages): Neil Corder
Photographer (cover): Neville Lockhart
Décor stylist: Tina Bester, Lisa Clark (cover)
Décor stylist's assistant: Michelle Haarhof
Food stylist: Justine Kiggen
Food stylist's assistants: Anke Roux, Erica Brown and Henrietta Madyum
Proofreader: Tessa Kennedy

Reproduction by Hirt & Carter Cape (Pty) Ltd
Printed and bound by Tien Wah Press (Pte) Limited, Singapore

ISBN 978-1-77007-762-1

www.imagesofafrica.co.za
IMAGES OF AFRICA
PHOTO LIBRARY

Over 40 000 unique African images available to purchase from our image
bank at **www.imagesofafrica.co.za**

AT MY TABLE
Fay Lewis

Coffee
AT MY TABLE

With the African bush as the backdrop use a combination of natural elements such as veld grass and quills with old black-and-white enamelware to create the perfect setting. Tins to hold sugar cubes and brown sugar may be wrapped in cream hessian and labelled with alphabet beads on a leather thong, and chocolate brown felt will keep the coffee pot warm. Add touches of colour with bright mohair blankets.

buttermilk *Rusks*

These rusks (on the left of the photograph) are delicious served straight from the oven (as soon as they've dried out) with home-made preserve – better than any scone you'll ever savour. Do not substitute margarine for the butter, as butter gives a far better taste.

MAKES 48 RUSKS

Preheat the oven to 190 °C. Combine the flour, sugar, baking powder, salt, cream of tartar and bicarbonate of soda in a large mixing bowl.

Add the remaining ingredients and mix and knead until the dough is soft and pliable.

Coat three loaf pans with cooking spray, or grease with butter or vegetable fat. Shape the dough into balls and place two balls side by side in rows into the prepared pans. Bake for 45 minutes or until a skewer inserted into the centre of the loaf comes out clean. Turn the loaf out onto a cooling rack and leave to cool.

Break the rusks into smaller pieces (do not cut with a knife). Dry out the rusks at 100 °C or in the warming drawer of the oven for 6–8 hours.

9 x 250 ml cake flour
375 ml white sugar
15 ml baking powder
5 ml salt
5 ml cream of tartar
7.5 ml bicarbonate of soda
500 ml buttermilk, sour cream
    or plain yoghurt
2 jumbo eggs
500 g butter, melted

Bran and Wholewheat Rusks

Follow the method for Buttermilk Rusks (above). As this dough is slightly sticky and less pliable, you will need to flour your hands when shaping the balls of dough.

Use the same ingredients as for the Buttermilk Rusks, but replace the 9 x 250 ml cake flour with:
6 x 250 ml wholewheat flour
2 x 250 ml muesli crunch
    cereal with raisins
2 x 250 ml All-Bran Flakes®
Substitute the white sugar with
    250 ml brown sugar

crunchie *Biscuits*

Oats are among the most nutritious of all the grains, and rolled oats have been used to make breakfast porridge for generations of families throughout the world. These biscuits are great with morning coffee and excellent to add as a healthy snack in a school lunchbox.

MAKES 30

Preheat the oven to 160 °C. Melt the syrup and the butter in a heavy-based saucepan.

Dissolve the bicarbonate of soda in the boiling water and add to the syrup and butter. Add the flour, oats, coconut and sugar and stir until combined.

Coat a lamington pan with cooking spray, or grease with butter or vegetable fat, and press the mixture into the pan. Bake for 35 minutes.

Switch off the oven, remove the pan and cut the biscuit into squares. Return the biscuits to the oven for 5 minutes to harden. Remove and leave to cool.

The clever cook can melt a 200 g slab of chocolate of their choice in a microwave oven on 50 per cent power, or in the top part of a double boiler over boiling water. Dip the tips of the cooled crunchies in the chocolate and keep aside until the chocolate has set.

50 ml golden syrup
300 g butter
10 ml bicarbonate of soda
100 ml boiling water
500 ml cake flour
500 ml oats
500 ml desiccated coconut
250 ml brown sugar

thin, crisp Chocolate Chip Cookies

These cookies are rich and buttery, with soft, tender centres and crisp edges.

MAKES 30

Preheat the oven to 180 °C. Sift the flour and the baking powder together in a small bowl and set aside.

Cream the butter, sugar and brown sugar together in an electric mixer until light and fluffy. Add the salt, vanilla essence, eggs and water. Beat until well mixed.

Spoon in the flour mixture and mix until just combined. Stir in the chocolate chips. Prepare four baking trays lined with baking paper and drop spoonfuls of the dough about 10 cm apart onto the prepared trays. Bake for 12–15 minutes or until the cookies are golden brown. Remove the cookies from the oven and cool on the baking trays for 1–2 minutes. Transfer to a wire rack, and let the cookies cool completely.

Store in an airtight container at room temperature for up to three weeks, IF there are still some left!

500 ml cake flour
5 ml baking powder
200 g unsalted butter
125 ml white sugar
200 ml brown sugar
5 ml salt
10 ml vanilla essence
2 jumbo eggs
60 ml water
500 ml dark or milk chocolate
    chips

apricot and pistachio *Biscotti*

Despite their elegant appearance, these twice-baked Italian biscuits are easy to make. A longer than average baking time produces a uniquely crunchy texture and also gives them an unusually long shelf life.

MAKES 30

To make the biscotti:
Preheat the oven to 180 °C. Cut the apricots in quarters and soak in the brandy for 30 minutes. Roast the pistachios on an unlined baking tray for 10 minutes. Cool and set aside.

Cream the butter and castor sugar in an electric mixer and add the beaten eggs. Mix thoroughly. Sift the flour, baking powder and salt together in a bowl and add to the butter and egg mixture. Combine to form a scone-like dough. Add the apricots, the left-over juices and the pistachios. Mix thoroughly.

Divide the dough into two or three equal parts on a lightly floured surface. Shape each piece of dough into a rectangle 20 x 8 cm and 2 cm thick.

To make the glaze:
Combine the milk and the egg yolk and brush the surfaces of the biscotti dough. Dust with the castor sugar.

Line a baking tray with baking paper and bake the biscotti for 30–40 minutes until slightly risen and golden brown.

Remove the biscotti from the oven and allow to cool for about 30 minutes before cutting into 1 cm thick slices. Arrange the biscotti on the racks of the oven and dry at 100 °C for 50–60 minutes.

Biscotti
150 g soft dried apricots
50 ml brandy
100 g whole pistachio nuts, shelled
100 g butter, softened
125 g castor sugar
2 jumbo eggs, beaten
350 g cake flour
7.5 ml baking powder
2.5 ml salt
extra flour for dusting surfaces
extra castor sugar for sprinkling

Glaze
50 ml milk
1 jumbo egg yolk

Kirsch and Brazil Nut Chocolate Biscotti

Use 300 g cake flour and 50 g cocoa powder. Use Kirsch liqueur instead of brandy and substitute the apricots with 150 g whole glacé cherries and the pistachios with 100 g chopped Brazil nuts. There is no need to roast the Brazil nuts. Follow the same method as above.

hot **Cinnamon Buns**

MAKES 14

Combine the flour, salt and sugar in a bowl. Add the yeast. Melt the butter in the milk in a small heavy-based saucepan, then set aside to cool.

Pour the milk mixture into the beaten eggs. Add the milk mixture to the flour and combine to form a soft, pliable dough. Knead the dough for about 10 minutes until the dough is smooth and elastic.

Place the dough on a lightly floured surface and cover with a sheet of clingfilm. Leave to rest for 20 minutes. Knock the dough down and divide into 14 equal pieces. Shape each piece into a ball and flatten into a 5 mm thick circle. Dust with half the sugar and cinnamon and sprinkle with a few sultanas.

Make one cut into each circle from the centre to the edge. Lift the dough on one cut side and fold it in half so that the fold forms a triangle. Fold over twice more so that you have three layers and a triangle bun.

Brush with the beaten egg and sprinkle the remaining sugar and cinnamon on top. Transfer onto two baking trays coated with cooking spray and cover with a sheet of clingfilm. Leave to prove for about 30 minutes or until doubled in size. Bake in a preheated oven at 200 °C for about 20 minutes or until golden brown.

600 g cake flour

10 ml salt

60 ml white sugar

1 x 10 g packet active dried yeast

125 g butter

250 ml milk

2 jumbo eggs, beaten

Topping/glaze

100 g white sugar and 5 ml cinnamon for dusting

100 g sultanas

1 jumbo egg, beaten

The best part of baking cinnamon buns is the heavenly aroma emanating from the oven.

If you like, you can make the dough the day before, refrigerate it overnight, then shape it,

allow it to rise and bake it the next day. This recipe also doubles easily.

perfect Pancakes

This is a flop-proof pancake mixture! You will turn out perfect batches in minutes. Ready-to-fry blintzes can be refrigerated for 1 day or frozen, filled, for three weeks. Unfilled blintzes can be frozen for up to two months.

MAKES 12 LARGE OR 18 SMALL

To make the pancakes:

Sift the flour and salt into a bowl. Beat the eggs, milk, cold water, melted butter and brandy together and add to the flour. Beat until smooth. If preferred, whisk all the ingredients together in a food processor fitted with a plastic blade.

Refrigerate the batter for at least 1 hour. Give the batter a stir and, if it seems too thick, add some more cold water until it is the consistency of thin cream. Heat a heavy-based frying pan and swirl the butter or oil around before pouring in a thin film of the batter. If you have poured in too much, pour the excess back into the jug. Once browned and set, flip the pancake over to lightly brown the other side.

To make the cheese filling:

Combine the cream cheese, flour and egg yolk in a bowl. Add the sugar and cinnamon.

To serve:

Place a spoon of filling on each pancake. Shape each pancake into a square and fry in heated cooking oil or butter until golden brown on both sides. Serve warm with a dollop of thick cream and cinnamon and sugar on the side.

thick cream and cinnamon-sugar for serving

Batter

250 ml cake flour
a pinch of salt
3 jumbo eggs
125 ml milk
125 ml cold water
15 ml melted butter or
   cooking oil
15 ml brandy

Cheese filling

250 g smooth cream cheese
15 ml cake flour
1 jumbo egg yolk
30 ml white sugar and
   cinnamon to taste

Cheesecake

SERVES 10

To make the pastry:
Combine the sugar and the flour in a bowl and rub in the butter. Add the egg. Mix into a pliable dough and press into a 24 cm springform pan coated with cooking spray, or greased with butter or vegetable fat. Place in the refrigerator for a couple of minutes.

To make the filling:
Preheat the oven to 180 °C. Combine all the ingredients in a food processor fitted with a plastic blade. Beat until thoroughly blended. Pour the filling into the unbaked pastry shell, then bake in the oven for 20 minutes. Switch off the oven and leave the cheesecake in the oven for 5–6 hours without opening the oven door.

Pastry
200 ml white sugar
500 ml self-raising flour
120 g butter
1 jumbo egg, beaten

Filling
3 x 250 g smooth cream cheese
250 ml fresh cream
4 jumbo eggs
50 ml custard powder
375 ml white sugar
5 ml vanilla essence
grated rind of 1 lemon

A good cheesecake is loved by all. Care must be taken while mixing the ingredients so that the filling does not contain lumps of unmixed cream cheese that can mar the smoothness of the baked cake. Frequent and thorough scraping of the bowl during mixing is key to ensuring that every spot of cream cheese is incorporated.

Four-by-Four Cake *with raspberries and blueberries*

SERVES 8–10

To make the cake:

Grease and flour a 23 cm springform pan and preheat the oven to 190 °C.

Break the eggs into a mixing bowl and add the sugar and the butter. Beat together using an electric mixer until the mixture is creamy. Add the flour and beat until smooth.

Spoon the mixture into the prepared pan. Toss two-thirds of the berries in the cake flour and scatter over the cake mixture. Bake for 45 minutes. Turn out onto a cake rack and allow to cool.

To serve:

Dust the cake with the icing sugar, then slice and serve with the remaining berries and the whipped cream.

* A four-by-four cake uses equal weights of eggs, butter, sugar and flour, i.e. if the 4 eggs weigh 60 g each, you will need 240 g of each of the remaining ingredients.

4 eggs, weighed in the shell
castor sugar*
butter*, softened
self-raising flour*
125 g punnet fresh raspberries
125 g punnet fresh blueberries
50 ml cake flour
icing sugar for dusting
250 ml fresh cream,
　　lightly whipped

Lemon Meringue *pie*

This is the ideal lemon meringue pie as it has a rich filling that balances the airy meringue without detracting from the flavour of the lemon.

SERVES 8–10

To make the base:

Crush the biscuits in a food processor fitted with a metal blade. Combine the crushed biscuits with the melted butter.

Line the sides and base of a 23 cm loose-base cake pan or a pie plate that has been coated with cooking spray, or greased with butter or vegetable fat. Place in the refrigerator for 15 minutes to set the crumbs.

To make the filling:

Preheat the oven to 160 °C. Combine the condensed milk, lemon juice and rind, and egg yolks in a bowl. Beat until thick.

In a separate bowl, whisk the egg whites with the salt until soft peak stage. Gradually add the castor sugar and icing sugar. Pour the condensed milk mixture into the biscuit base and spoon the meringue mixture on top. Bake at 160 °C for 20 minutes, then reduce the oven temperature to 120 °C and bake for another 10 minutes or until the meringue is set. Allow to cool.

The clever cook should bake and serve the lemon meringue on the same day. If you need to prepare it a day in advance, be sure to refrigerate it – this will prevent the meringue from 'weeping'.

Base

2 x 200 g packets Tennis biscuits
120 g butter, melted

Filling

3 x 385 g cans condensed milk
juice and rind of 3 lemons
4 jumbo eggs, separated
5 ml salt
60 ml castor sugar
60 ml icing sugar

triple chocolate chip *Cookies*

Three kinds of chocolate combine to make these cookies the richest you've ever eaten – but oh so yummy! These cookies are thick right from the edge to the centre and are chewy, but soft.

MAKES 25

Preheat the oven to 170 °C. Melt the dark and the milk chocolate in a heavy-based saucepan over a low heat. Add the butter and stir gently until melted.

Combine the flour, baking powder, salt and cinnamon in a bowl and set aside. In a separate bowl, beat the eggs, coffee powder and vanilla together until frothy.

Gradually add the sugar and beat until the mixture is light and creamy in colour. Beat in the melted chocolate mixture, then fold in the flour mixture. Stir in the nuts, if using, and the chocolate chips.

Line three baking trays with baking paper. Drop teaspoonfuls of the batter onto the baking trays leaving about 6 cm between the cookies.

Bake one tray at a time for 10–12 minutes. When ready, the tops should be cracked and the centres soft. Remove the cookies from the oven and cool on the baking tray for about 3 minutes. Using a spatula, transfer the cookies to a cooling rack. Cool completely, then store in an airtight container.

200 g dark chocolate
100 g milk chocolate
100 g butter, cut into pieces
100 ml cake flour
5 ml baking powder
a pinch of salt
2.5 ml ground cinnamon
2 jumbo eggs
10 ml instant coffee powder
10 ml vanilla essence
150 g white sugar
100 g pecan nuts, coarsely chopped (optional)
100 g walnuts, coarsely chopped (optional)
200 g chocolate chips

Brunch

AT MY TABLE

Long, lazy brunches in the summer sun and the sound

of the waves tumbling in the background are enough

to make anyone want to live by the sea. Using a

combination of indigo voile, contemporary cream

crockery and a mish-mash of chairs and benches,

a relaxed setting is created to make guests feel at home.

Shell mobiles waft in the breeze and driftwood and

mussel shells make the perfect table setting accessories.

fruity *Muesli*

This muesli ensures a calming start to any hectic day. I always suggest it to my girls for the morning before an important examination as it's real brain food! Any fruit is great in this recipe. In summer I include a combination of peach and mango and top the bowl with a heap of raspberries.

SERVES 8

To make the muesli:
Combine the oats, juice and yoghurt in a large bowl. Cover tightly and refrigerate overnight. Stir the dates, raisins, apricots, honey, milk and apple into the oat mixture. Cover and return to the refrigerator for 30 minutes.

The clever cook should use plain full-cream yoghurt for this recipe. Other types, especially low fat, are not suitable. Additional milk can be added if the muesli is too thick. Use a tart, crisp green apple, such as a Granny Smith, for this recipe.

To serve:
Serve the muesli in individual serving bowls, topped with the almonds and mixed berries.

750 ml rolled oats

500 ml fresh orange juice

500 ml plain yoghurt

250 ml seeded and chopped
dried dates

125 ml seedless raisins

125 ml thinly sliced
dried apricots

100 ml honey

250 ml milk

1 large apple, peeled and
coarsely grated

100 ml toasted slivered
almonds and fresh mixed
berries for serving

toasted *Muesli*

My family doesn't like nuts, but you are welcome to add some chopped pecans or cashew nuts. Don't use walnuts as these can make the muesli 'bitter'.

SERVES 4

500 ml rolled oats
125 ml unprocessed bran
125 ml finely chopped dried apricots
125 ml finely chopped dried apples
125 ml sultanas
30 ml honey
50 ml water

To make the muesli:
Preheat the oven to 150 °C. Combine the oats, bran and dried fruit in a medium-sized bowl. Combine the honey and water and stir into the oat mixture.

Spread the mixture onto a non-stick oven tray and bake in the oven for 45 minutes or until toasted, stirring occasionally. Remove and allow to cool.

When required, serve the muesli with plain yoghurt and extra chopped dried apricots.

The clever cook can double or treble the recipe and refrigerate the muesli in an airtight container for several weeks.

A brioche is a soft roll made from a yeast dough enriched with butter and eggs. It is best served warm with lashings of butter and honey or fruit preserve. It is also delicious toasted or used as a case for cooked savoury food such as seafood or mushrooms.

Brioches

MAKES 16

Sprinkle the yeast over the warm water in a large mixing bowl and stir until dissolved. Add the sugar, salt, lemon rind, butter, eggs and flour. Mix to form a soft dough.

Cover the bowl with clingfilm and place in a warm spot, covered with a blanket for 1 hour, or until the dough has doubled in bulk. Refrigerate overnight.

Make 16 large and 16 small balls from the dough and place the larger balls in muffin pans coated with cooking spray. Make an indentation in each large ball and brush with the egg yolk. Place a smaller ball on top of each larger ball.

Allow to rise until double in bulk or for about 1 hour. Preheat the oven to 180 °C. Add the water to the remaining egg yolk and brush the brioches with the egg mixture. Bake for 15–20 minutes or until golden brown.

1 x 10 g packet active dried yeast
125 ml warm water
70 ml white sugar
5 ml salt
5 ml grated lemon rind
230 g butter, softened
6 jumbo eggs
5 x 250 ml cake flour
1 jumbo egg yolk, lightly beaten
15 ml water

Cinnamon-Buttermilk Pancakes
with glazed pears

MAKES 16 PANCAKES

To make the glazed pears:
Combine the red wine, castor sugar, water and lemon juice in a large heavy-based frying pan. Stir over low heat until the sugar dissolves.

Add the pear slices in a single layer and simmer, turning occasionally, over medium heat for 20–25 minutes until the syrup is thick and the pears are glazed. Transfer to a bowl and leave to cool.

To make the pancakes:
Combine the buttermilk, ricotta and egg yolks in a bowl and whisk until combined.

Sift the flour, bicarbonate of soda and cinnamon into a separate bowl. Gradually whisk the flour mixture into the buttermilk mixture to form a thick, smooth batter.

Whisk the egg whites until soft peaks form, then gradually add the castor sugar and whisk until stiff. Using a large metal spoon, mix half the egg white mixture into the pancake batter. Add the remaining egg white mixture and fold it in gently.

Heat the cooking oil in a non-stick heavy-based frying pan. Add spoonfuls of pancake batter, cook for 2–3 minutes over medium heat until the underside is golden, then flip and cook for 2–3 minutes more or until the pancake is cooked and puffed. Remove, cover and keep warm in a low oven. Repeat with the remaining pancake mixture.

To serve:
Serve the pancakes immediately, topped with a little mascarpone and the pear slices and drizzled with the pear syrup.

The clever cook can substitute the pears for peaches or any other firm, seasonal fruit.

Glazed pears
250 ml red wine
250 ml castor sugar
120 ml water
15 ml fresh lemon juice
4 firm pears, peeled, cored and cut into 8 slices each

Pancakes
200 ml buttermilk
250 g ricotta cheese, crumbled
4 jumbo eggs, separated
250 ml self-raising flour
2.5 ml bicarbonate of soda
5 ml ground cinnamon
60 ml castor sugar
50 ml cooking oil for frying
mascarpone to serve

While preparing these pancakes your kitchen will be filled with a mouthwatering cinnamon aroma. The combination of ricotta cheese, cinnamon and mascarpone will take the taste sensation to new heights! I have also served this dish as a winter dessert.

day before Muffins

These muffins are a favourite of my daughter Marissa – nutritious and tasty and an excellent way to add fibre to your diet.

MAKES 8

To make the muffins:
Combine the chopped apricots, figs, cereal, milk, sugar and syrup in a large bowl. Cover and refrigerate overnight.

Preheat the oven to 200 °C. Coat eight cups of a 180 ml size muffin pan with cooking spray, or grease with butter or vegetable fat. Stir the flour and nuts into the apricot mixture, then spoon into the sprayed muffin pan. Bake for 30 minutes or until the muffins are golden brown.

To serve:
Serve hot or cold, with sifted icing sugar and topped with dried apricots.

The clever cook can wrap these muffins individually in clingfilm, or store in an airtight plastic container and freeze for up to 2 months.

200 ml coarsely chopped
   dried apricots
125 ml coarsely chopped
   dried figs
350 ml All-Bran Flakes®
375 ml milk
250 ml brown sugar
15 ml golden syrup
350 ml self-raising flour
125 ml coarsely chopped
   pecan nuts
icing sugar and extra dried
   apricots for serving

Marissa's anytime *Bran Muffins*

MAKES 15 JUMBO

Preheat the oven to 200 °C. Coat the number of muffin cups you plan to use with cooking spray, or line them with paper cupcake liners.

Combine the flour, baking powder and salt in a very large bowl. Place the cereal in a separate bowl, pour over the boiling water and leave to soak.

Combine the butter and honey in a large bowl. Beat the eggs in a separate bowl and stir in the buttermilk. Combine the buttermilk mixture with the honey/butter mixture.

Add the flour mixture and stir gently by hand until well mixed. Fold in the bran, soaked cereal flakes, raisins and chopped nuts. DO NOT stir.

Spoon the batter into the muffin cups, filling them to two-thirds full, and bake for 25–35 minutes, depending on the size of the muffin pan.

Store any unused batter in an airtight container in the refrigerator or freezer. When next using the batter, spoon it directly into the muffin cups without stirring the mixture.

The clever cook can pour water into each empty muffin cup to allow for even baking, and to keep the oven moist during the baking process. This also prevents the muffin pan from warping.

6 x 250 ml wholewheat flour
25 ml baking powder
5 ml salt
500 ml cereal flakes, e.g. bran or muesli (the muesli will result in a sweeter muffin)
500 ml boiling water
250 ml melted butter
250 ml honey
4 jumbo eggs
250 ml buttermilk
500 ml unprocessed bran
125 ml raisins or chopped dates or currants
125 ml chopped nuts (optional)

Good hot with butter, or plain. This recipe is suitable for mixing in bulk and storing in an airtight container, in the refrigerator, for several weeks. You will need a LARGE bowl. Of course, if you plan to use it all at once, you will require a commercial oven, or the help of your neighbours on both sides!

wholewheat *Bread*

There is nothing better than the aroma of freshly baked bread. This wholewheat loaf is delicious served fresh from the oven with lashings of butter and home-made preserves. Or try it toasted and serve with the Scrambled Eggs on page 55.

MAKES 1 LOAF OR 8 MUFFINS

Spoon the honey and yeast into 100 ml of the warm water and leave to rise for 5 minutes in a warm spot.*

Mix together the nutty wheat, rolled oats, crushed wheat, oil and salt. Add the yeast mixture and the rest of the water and blend together.

Spoon into a greased, medium loaf pan or muffin pan, allowing sufficient space for proving. Sprinkle the sunflower seeds, sesame seeds and linseed on top.

Place the pan in a warm spot for 40 minutes then bake the loaf at 200 °C for about 45 minutes. (If using a muffin pan bake for 20 minutes.)

The clever cook can insert a skewer into the centre of the loaf. If the skewer comes out clean, the bread is baked.

* The warming drawer of the oven is a suitable proving spot. Alternatively, cover the pan with foil and a blanket.

25 ml honey
1 x 10 g packet active
    dried yeast
800 ml warm water
4 x 250 ml nutty wheat flour
250 ml rolled oats
250 ml crushed wheat
15 ml cooking oil
15 ml salt
50 ml sunflower or
    pumpkin seeds
50 ml sesame seeds
50 ml linseed

fresh farm **Salad**

SERVES 4

To make the salad:

Wash the salad leaves and lettuce hearts in cold water. Shake or spin dry. Wrap loosely in a tea towel and place in the refrigerator to chill.

Poach the vegetable strips in lightly salted water until just tender. Drain and chill.

To make the dressing:

Combine the balsamic vinegar, mustard and sugar in a small bowl. Whisk in the olive oil and chives and season to taste with the salt, pepper and chillies.

To serve:

Toss the salad leaves and poached vegetables in the dressing and arrange on individual chilled salad plates. Top each salad with lettuce hearts and garnish with cherry tomatoes, spring onion, basil and parmesan shavings. Spoon over the remaining dressing and serve immediately.

Use only young, tender, fresh greens, vegetables and fruit when making salads and assemble just prior to serving, adding the dressing at the last minute.

Salad

12 baby rocket leaves
12 crisp iceberg lettuce leaves
4 round lettuce hearts
4 red oak leaf lettuce hearts
12 julienne strips of carrot
12 julienne strips of yellow
    courgette (baby marrow)
12 julienne strips of green
    courgette (baby marrow)

Dressing

60 ml balsamic vinegar
10 ml Dijon mustard
5 ml castor sugar
120 ml extra virgin olive oil
60 ml finely snipped
    fresh chives
salt and freshly ground
    black pepper
crushed dried chillies

Garnish

orange, red and yellow
    cherry tomatoes
chopped spring onions
sprigs of fresh basil
parmesan cheese shavings

Tomato, Mozzarella and Basil Stack
with balsamic and lime vinaigrette

SERVES 4

To make the dressing:
Combine the olive oil, balsamic vinegar, lemon juice and castor sugar in a sealable container. Add the slivered basil leaves and season to taste with the salt, pepper and chillies. Mix well, then add the sliced mozzarella, spooning the dressing over the slices. Leave in the refrigerator to marinate until ready to serve.

To make the salad stack:
Cut the tomatoes, including the tops and bottoms, into 6 mm thick slices. (If preferred, don't cut the slices all the way through, keeping the tomatoes intact.) Stack the slices together to re-form each tomato.

Using a slotted spoon, remove the marinated slices of mozzarella from the dressing (reserve the dressing). Alternate slices of tomato and mozzarella to create a stack on each plate, adding a leaf or two of basil to each layer of cheese and ending each stack with a tomato 'cap'.

Spoon the dressing over. Garnish each plate with a sprig of basil and a few olives and serve immediately.

Balsamic and lime vinaigrette
150 ml extra virgin olive oil
30 ml balsamic vinegar
45 ml fresh lemon juice
5 ml castor sugar
fresh basil leaves, cut into thin slivers
salt and freshly ground black pepper
crushed dried chillies

Salad stack
16 thin slices of buffalo mozzarella
4 large, ripe tomatoes, chilled
16–24 fresh basil leaves

Garnish
4 sprigs of fresh basil
black olives

This towering salad of tomato, mozzarella and basil leaves, served with a vinaigrette of balsamic vinegar, lime and basil, is best made when vine-ripened tomatoes are available in the supermarkets.

red onion, cheese and vegetable *Frittata*

A frittata is just a fancy Italian term for an open omelette. This vegetable combination is absolutely delicious served as part of a brunch menu or for a light Sunday supper.

SERVES 4

Heat the oil in a 23 cm non-stick frying pan. Sauté the onions and garlic until soft. Stir in the courgettes and mushrooms. Cook, stirring, until the vegetables are tender. Stir in the herbs and pepper.

Reduce the heat and pour in the eggs. Cook the egg mixture over low heat, without stirring, until the base is lightly browned and the top is almost set. Sprinkle with the cheese.

Place the pan under the grill set on high heat, until the top is set and lightly browned. Cut into wedges. Serve warm with a fresh garden salad.

The clever cook can serve this recipe directly from the frying pan. This dish is best made just prior to serving.

30 ml olive oil
2 red onions, thinly sliced
1 clove garlic, crushed
2 large courgettes (baby marrows), grated
250 g button mushrooms, thinly sliced
15 ml snipped fresh chives
30 ml chopped fresh basil
5 ml freshly ground black pepper
8 jumbo eggs, lightly beaten
250 ml grated mozzarella cheese

Scrambled Eggs *with a difference*

Serve this combination of creamy scrambled eggs (free-range eggs yield the best result) and smoked salmon on wholewheat toast.

SERVES 4

Place the eggs in a small bowl with the milk and chives. Whisk to combine.

Melt the butter in a medium-size heavy-based saucepan over low heat. Fry the onions until glossy, then add the egg mixture. When the egg starts to 'catch' on the bottom of the pan, stir continuously with a wooden spoon until the egg is just firm.

Serve with wholewheat toast and smoked salmon and sprinkle with chives or spring onions.

The clever cook can whisk the eggs just long enough to combine the yolks and whites. Excessive beating will aerate the mixture too much. Cook the eggs just before serving. Any suitable chopped herb or chopped red onion can be substituted for the chives.

8 jumbo eggs, lightly beaten
100 ml milk or fresh cream
30 ml snipped fresh chives
30 ml butter
2 onions, finely chopped
extra snipped chives or
    chopped spring onions
    to garnish

snoek and caper *Quiche*

MAKES 6 SLICES OR 3 INDIVIDUAL SERVINGS

To make the pastry:

Sift the flour and salt together. Grate the butter and, using your fingertips, rub it into the flour until crumbly. Add the water and the cream cheese and mix to a soft consistency.

Place the pastry on a floured board and knead lightly before shaping into a smooth ball. Wrap in clingfilm and place in the refrigerator for 2 hours.

When ready, preheat the oven to 200 °C. Roll out the pastry and line a large 23 cm quiche dish or single-serve 13 cm quiche pans. Bake blind for 8–9 minutes. Remove from the oven.

To make the filling:

Reduce the oven temperature to 180 °C. Scatter the snoek and cheeses over the base of the cooked pastry case.

Heat the cooking oil in a small heavy-based frying pan and fry the leeks. Scatter the cooked leeks over the cheese and snoek mixture. Mix together the remaining ingredients and pour over the snoek.

Bake at 180 °C for 50 minutes for the large quiche, or about 30 minutes for the smaller quiches. Serve warm.

The clever cook can use smoked angelfish or tuna instead of snoek for a tasty alternative.

This quiche is great for brunch as well as for supper – serve with a mixed green salad and some crusty bread. The aged cheddar combined with the smoked fish gives this quiche a wonderful flavour!

Pastry

240 g cake flour
2.5 ml salt
120 g butter (straight from the refrigerator)
50 ml ice-cold water
100 g smooth cream cheese

Filling

200 g flaked smoked snoek
250 ml grated mature cheddar cheese
250 ml grated mozzarella cheese
30 ml cooking oil
3 leeks, white part only, sliced
4 jumbo eggs
375 ml fresh cream
125 ml sour cream
a pinch of freshly ground black pepper
5 ml prepared English mustard
30 ml fresh lemon juice
50 ml chopped capers
30 ml chopped fresh parsley

smoked beef and artichoke *Quiche*

If you are a ware Suid-Afrikaner *(a true South African), I suggest you use some biltong instead of the smoked beef. If you are an expat tuning in from Atlanta, USA, pop down to your deli for some jerky. Unfortunately, I cannot oblige with the African Sunset…*

MAKES 1 LARGE

To make the pastry:

Sift the flour and salt together. Add the chives. Grate the butter and, using your fingertips, rub it into the flour until crumbly. Add the water and mix to a soft consistency.

Place the pastry on a floured board and knead lightly before shaping into a smooth ball. Wrap in clingfilm and place in the refrigerator for 2 hours.

When ready, preheat the oven to 200 °C. Roll out the pastry and line a 23 cm quiche dish. Bake blind for 8–9 minutes. Remove from the oven.

To make the filling:

Reduce the oven temperature to 180 °C. Heat the oil in a heavy-based frying pan and sauté the spring onions, smoked beef and artichoke slices.

Remove the mixture from the frying pan and scatter it over the pastry case, followed by the cheeses. Mix together the remaining ingredients and pour over the smoked beef mixture. Bake at 180 °C for 45 minutes. Serve warm.

The clever cook can substitute bamboo shoots for the artichokes, if preferred.

Pastry

160 g cake flour
2.5 ml salt
15 ml snipped fresh chives
120 g butter
50 ml ice-cold water
   (if necessary)

Filling

30 ml cooking oil
4 spring onions, chopped
150 g smoked beef or turkey,
   chopped
1 x 440 g can artichoke hearts,
   drained and thinly sliced
250 ml grated cheddar cheese
250 ml grated mozzarella
   cheese
3 jumbo eggs
250 ml fresh cream
125 ml sour cream
a pinch each of salt and freshly
   ground black pepper
5 ml mustard powder
15 ml fresh lemon juice
5 ml grated lemon rind

Champagne *fruits*

Champagne at brunch time can be addictive, especially when it is the fizzing ingredient of a fresh-tasting fruit salad.

SERVES 4

Peel the pineapple, core and slice into rings. Slice each ring in half and combine with the pears, apples, plums, bananas, grapes and apricots in a mixing bowl. Dust with icing sugar to taste, moisten with the brandy and lemon juice, toss and chill.

To serve:
When ready to serve, transfer the fruit to a serving bowl, and pour the champagne over.

The clever cook can use a variety of canned fruits as a substitute for the fresh fruit – canned baby apples add an aesthetic touch!

1 medium pineapple
4 pears, peeled, cored
    and sliced
4 crisp apples, peeled, cored
    and sliced
4 plums, stoned and sliced
4 bananas, peeled and sliced
1 bunch of grapes, halved
    and seeded
4 apricots, halved and stoned
icing sugar for dusting
30 ml brandy
30 ml fresh lemon juice
250 ml champagne or
    sparkling wine

mango or strawberry *Smoothie*

Blend luscious summer fruits such as melons, mangoes or strawberries into creamy smoothies.

MAKES 1 LITRE

Place all the ingredients into a blender and purée until smooth. Chill the mixture in the refrigerator for 1 hour. Stir the mixture and pour into tall glasses before serving.

The clever cook can substitute the mangoes with 800 g strawberries and increase the amount of sugar if the strawberries are tart to the taste.

2 ripe mangoes, peeled, stone removed, and roughly chopped
250 ml plain yoghurt
30 ml white sugar

Honeyed Yoghurt *with fresh berries*

SERVES 4

Place the yoghurt and 45 ml of honey in a bowl and mix well. Spoon into glasses or bowls and top with the berries. Drizzle over the remaining honey and top with a sprig of mint.

The clever cook can stir 5 ml vanilla essence into each 250 ml of yoghurt for a delicious vanilla flavour.

750 ml Greek-style full-cream
  yoghurt
50 ml honey
250 ml mixed berries
fresh mint to decorate

This is more a reminder than a recipe! A reminder that thick, creamy yoghurt goes well with honey and any luscious fruit. My husband Leon enjoys this mixture with sliced mango, and my girls, when feeling peckish mid-afternoon, often fill a tea cup, grab a teaspoon and disappear into their rooms…

Oranges and Prunes *in orange tea syrup*

SERVES 4

To make the prunes:

Soak the prunes, orange rind and tea bag in boiling water for 20 minutes, or until the prunes are plump. Remove the tea bag and drain the prunes and the orange rind, reserving the liquid.

To make the orange syrup:

Combine the sugar, cinnamon sticks, orange juice and liquid from the prunes in a medium heavy-based saucepan and bring to the boil. Lower the heat and simmer for 5 minutes.

Add the peppercorns, drained prunes and orange rind, and cook for a further 10 minutes. Remove from the heat.

To serve:

Arrange the orange slices in long-stemmed glasses and add the prunes and hot orange syrup. Leave to cool. Chill until ready to serve.

3 navel oranges, peeled
 and sliced

Prunes

250 g large prunes, pitted
4 strips thinly pared
 orange rind
1 orange tea bag
 (commercially available)
sufficient boiling water to cover

Orange syrup

100 g white sugar
2–3 sticks cinnamon
150 ml fresh orange juice
liquid reserved from prunes
15 ml pink peppercorns

This amber-tinted, tea-scented concoction makes the perfect morning eye-opener for a great breakfast. Young and old will enjoy this healthy beginning to the day!

red and blue *Fruit Bowl*

This brilliantly coloured summer fruit salad – a stunning combination of reds and blues – makes a great morning 'freshener'. Choose perfectly ripe fruit and serve chilled with a dollop of crème fraîche.* I also serve this as a summer dinner party dessert.

SERVES 4

Pit the cherries, hull the strawberries and strip the stems from the redcurrants. Clean the fruits as necessary and combine them in a bowl. Flavour the lemon juice with cognac and icing sugar to taste. Add the flavoured lemon juice to the fruit and toss lightly. Marinate in the refrigerator for at least 30 minutes. Dust with icing sugar just before serving.

* Crème fraîche is readily available in leading supermarkets. You can easily prepare your own by combining 250 ml fresh cream with 15 ml full-cream natural yoghurt or buttermilk. Chill in the refrigerator. The mixture will thicken as it chills.

The clever cook can use any combination of seasonal berries – whatever is readily available.

225 g dark red cherries
1 x 500 g punnet strawberries
1 x 200 g punnet redcurrants
1 x 200 g punnet raspberries
1 x 200 g punnet blueberries
juice of 2 lemons
a little cognac
icing sugar to taste and extra
    for dusting
crème fraîche for serving

Lunch
AT MY TABLE

The first days of spring

call for long lunches – alfresco – with chilled asparagus

soup and delicious barbecued red roman. Brighten your

table with ranunculus, cotton cushions and bright pencils

tied up like butterflies with pipe cleaners. Bring a touch

of fantasy to your garden with pinwheels in party pinks

and brilliant orange and hang spring flowers on striped

ribbons from the trees.

Deep-fried King Prawns *with Leon's favourite red rice*

I get cleaned prawns from the fishmonger, but if you are going to clean them yourself, snap off the heads and, using a sharp pair of scissors, cut down the back of each prawn, pull out the dark thread and discard it. Rinse under cold running water and pat dry.

SERVES 4

To prepare the prawns:

Season the prawns with the garlic, lemon juice, sea salt and pepper.

Heat 10 cm of cooking oil in a deep-fryer or 5 cm of cooking oil in a heavy-based saucepan until hot. Drop four prawns at a time into the heated cooking oil for 1–2 minutes or until the shells of the prawns turn opaque in colour. Drain on paper towelling and continue with the remaining prawns. Place the cooked prawns in a casserole dish in a preheated oven at 100 °C until ready to serve. Sprinkle with the parsley and chives.

The clever cook can also bake or grill the prawns.

For grilling: Brush the prawns with 125 g butter (melted), season and grill under the preheated grill of the oven for 5 minutes or until cooked.

For baking: Melt 125 g butter in a shallow baking pan and add the seasoned prawns. Bake at 200 °C for 5 minutes.

20 king prawns, cleaned and deveined
3 cloves garlic, crushed
75 ml fresh lemon juice
coarse sea salt and freshly ground black pepper
oil for deep-frying
15 ml chopped fresh parsley
15 ml snipped fresh chives

Leon's favourite red rice

Melt the butter in a medium heavy-based saucepan and sauté the rice, leeks, red, yellow and green peppers, and celery until the peppers and celery are tender. Add the tomatoes, wine and stock and simmer, uncovered, until tender. Add a little extra stock if necessary. Season to taste. The rice must be moist and almost have the texture of paella.

The clever cook can use any left-over vegetables – I always use the bits and pieces I have in my refrigerator.

50 g butter
500 ml long grain rice
3 leeks, white part only, sliced
1 red pepper, cut into strips
1 yellow pepper, cut into strips
1 green pepper, cut into strips
6 stalks celery, cut into strips
1x 400 g can chopped tomatoes
250 ml dry white wine
250 ml vegetable stock
salt and freshly ground black pepper

Barbecued Red Roman *with herbed mayonnaise*

SERVES 4

To prepare the fish:

Ask your fishmonger to clean and scale the fish and to remove the backbone, but leave the head and tail intact. Slash three deep cuts into both fleshy sides. Season inside and out with the salt, pepper, lemon juice and garlic. Place the mixed herbs inside the belly of the fish. Oil the fish skin and grid with the olive oil and barbecue over medium-hot coals, allowing 15 minutes on each side. While the fish is cooking, make the mayonnaise.

To make the mayonnaise:

Combine the eggs, 200 ml of the cooking oil, the lemon juice or vinegar, mustard powder, sugar, salt and white pepper in a food processor fitted with a plastic blade. Put the lid on and turn the motor to high. When blended, remove the cover and add the remaining 300 ml oil in a thin, steady trickle, blending continuously. Adjust the seasoning and add the chives.

To serve:

Test whether the fish is cooked by slicing the flesh at the thickest part with a small, sharp knife. The flesh should be opaque all the way through. Transfer the fish to a large serving platter and garnish with the lemon wedges and fresh herbs. Serve immediately with the herbed mayonnaise.

2 red romans (each about 25 cm in length)
salt and freshly ground black pepper
juice of 1 lemon
2 cloves garlic, crushed
50 ml chopped mixed fresh herbs
100 ml olive oil for the fish skin and the grid

Herbed mayonnaise
2 jumbo eggs
500 ml cooking oil
60 ml fresh lemon juice or white vinegar
2.5 ml mustard powder
10 ml castor sugar
a pinch of salt
freshly ground white pepper
15 ml snipped fresh chives

Garnish
lemon wedges
fresh herbs

Nothing is quite as delicious as a whole fish barbecued over open coals. If the weather makes it impossible to barbecue, place the fish in a roasting pan, moisten with a little white wine and cover with aluminium foil. Bake in a preheated oven at 180 °C for 50–60 minutes or until the fish is cooked through.

Avocado and Rocket Salad *with a curry dressing*

This salad is perfect with roasted meat or grilled fish. The small amount of curry powder gives a subtle spiciness that does not overwhelm the dressing.

SERVES 4

Halve the avocado and remove the stone. Peel the flesh and slice lengthways. Wash the tomatoes, cut each tomato into eight segments and remove the seeds. Combine the vinegar, sugar, curry powder, salt, pepper and olive oil in a salad bowl.

Gently toss the avocado, tomatoes and olives in the dressing just before serving. Add the rocket leaves and toss gently again.

1 just-ripe avocado
2 large ripe tomatoes
60 ml balsamic vinegar
30 ml brown sugar
2.5 ml curry powder
salt and freshly ground
    black pepper
60 ml extra virgin olive oil
10 black olives
250 g washed and dried
    rocket leaves

Pasta with roasted cherry tomatoes and fresh basil

SERVES 4

Preheat the oven to 200 °C. Place the tomato halves in a large baking dish that can be brought to the table. In a small bowl, combine the garlic, breadcrumbs, cheese, salt and pepper. Spoon the mixture evenly over the tomatoes, then spoon the olive oil evenly over the mixture. Roast the tomatoes for 30–35 minutes or until the mixture is bubbly, browned and slightly thickened. Cook the pasta in a large heavy-based saucepan of salted boiling water. Drain well. Add the pasta to the tomato mixture in the baking dish. Toss to combine. Scatter the basil over and serve immediately.

The clever cook can add shredded cooked chicken to the pasta for a more substantial dish, or refrigerate any leftover pasta and serve chilled the next day with cold roast chicken or salmon.

800 g ripe cherry tomatoes, halved
4 cloves garlic, crushed
125 ml fresh white breadcrumbs
60 g parmesan cheese, grated
salt and freshly ground black pepper
60 ml olive oil
500 g rigatoni or penne
125 ml fresh basil leaves

Rustic in flavour and presentation, this dish is delicious.

You can never have too many caramelised tomatoes

on plain pasta!

Linguine *ortobosco*

SERVES 6

Boil the pasta in salted water in a large heavy-based saucepan until al dente. Drain the pasta and set aside. Heat the olive oil in a large, heavy-based frying pan and sauté the garlic. Add the green pepper, onion, carrot and celery and fry, stirring continuously, for 5 minutes. Add the wine, mushrooms and baby marrow and simmer for another 5 minutes. Add the tomatoes and chilli and simmer until all the excess liquid has evaporated. Add the rosemary and basil and season to taste with the salt and pepper. Toss the cooked pasta into the sauce and simmer over low heat for 1 minute. Sprinkle with the grated parmesan and top with a sprig of basil. Serve immediately.

500 g linguine
150 ml olive oil
2 cloves garlic, crushed
1 green pepper, seeded and finely chopped
1 onion, chopped
3 carrots, finely chopped
6 stalks celery, chopped
250 ml dry white wine
250 g fresh porcini or button mushrooms
300 g courgettes (baby marrows), sliced
1 x 410 g can whole peeled Italian tomatoes
5 ml chopped fresh chilli
50 ml chopped fresh rosemary
50 ml chopped fresh basil
salt and freshly ground black pepper
grated parmesan cheese and sprigs of basil to garnish

Mastrantonio Illovo is our favourite family restaurant. My girls often say that the food and the service is better than at home! This is my favourite dish from their very extensive menu and the dish definitely tastes better when Paolo is in attendance!

Oriental Vegetables *in coconut cream*

This recipe dresses up vegetables with a subtly flavoured coconut cream to create a light vegetarian dish of distinction. This dish is also an excellent accompaniment to skewers of poultry or fish with basmati rice.

SERVES 4

Heat the cooking oil in a large heavy-based frying pan and stir-fry the onion and garlic until softened. Add the mangetout, peas and carrots and season with the turmeric, chilli powder and salt. Add 150 ml of the coconut milk and cook for 3 minutes, stirring constantly. Add the cabbage and tomatoes and cook for a further 3 minutes. Pour in the remaining coconut milk and simmer for 1–2 minutes so that the vegetables are hot but crunchy. Taste and adjust the seasoning. Serve immediately.

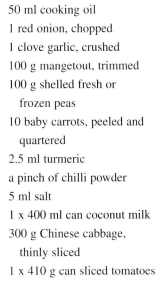

50 ml cooking oil

1 red onion, chopped

1 clove garlic, crushed

100 g mangetout, trimmed

100 g shelled fresh or
    frozen peas

10 baby carrots, peeled and
    quartered

2.5 ml turmeric

a pinch of chilli powder

5 ml salt

1 x 400 ml can coconut milk

300 g Chinese cabbage,
    thinly sliced

1 x 410 g can sliced tomatoes

Mango Chicken *with macadamia nuts*

SERVES 4

Stir-fry the chicken in batches in the heated cooking oil in a large heavy-based frying pan or wok. Remove the chicken and set aside.

Add the onions and the peppers and stir-fry until soft. Add the wine, garlic, chilli, basil and salt. Bring to the boil.

Return the chicken to the pan. Add the mangoes and rocket. Stir until the rocket is just wilted. Pile the chicken mixture onto a platter and top with the nuts.

The clever cook can use papino if mangoes are out of season.

8 chicken thighs, deboned, skinned and thinly sliced
50 ml cooking oil
2 onions, sliced
2 yellow peppers, seeded and sliced
1 red pepper, seeded and sliced
50 ml dry white wine
1 clove garlic, crushed
1 small fresh red chilli, seeded and chopped
15 ml chopped fresh basil
5 ml salt
2 mangoes, peeled, stoned and finely sliced (or use canned)
60 g rocket
100 g toasted chopped macadamia nuts

I love the flavour and taste of roasted macadamia nuts so I always have to toast more than double those required for the recipe as I munch my way through them. The macadamias remind me of wonderful vacations we have spent in the Lowveld and the Sabi Sand Game Reserve, where you can always enjoy these nuts with drinks while watching the setting African sun.

Spanish *Chicken*

This is a favourite of mine going back to my days at the University of Cape Town. The sauce is tangy, but not too spicy, and all your guests will ask what gives this dish that special taste. Nobody will guess that it is the curry powder!

SERVES 4

Preheat the oven to 180 °C. Brown the chicken pieces in the heated cooking oil in a heavy-based frying pan and season with the salt and pepper.

Combine all the remaining ingredients, except the rocket, in a heavy-based saucepan and boil for 10 minutes. Place the browned chicken pieces in a casserole dish coated with cooking spray, or greased with butter or vegetable fat, and pour the sauce over. Bake for 1–1½ hours. Garnish with wild rocket and serve with buttered peas and rice.

1 chicken, cut into 8 portions
50 ml cooking oil
5 ml sea salt crystals
2.5 ml freshly ground
    black pepper
2 x 400 g cans tomato soup
30 ml brown vinegar
30 ml brown sugar
100 ml chutney
1 onion, chopped
1 green pepper, seeded
    and chopped
250 ml chopped fresh parsley
15 ml curry powder of your
    choice (I prefer mild)
2 x 285 g cans whole or sliced
    button mushrooms, drained
wild rocket to garnish

roasted *Lamb Shanks*

I serve this dish at almost every Friday night supper. It only takes a couple of minutes to prepare – the oven takes care of the rest of the job! The lamb needs to cook until perfectly tender and should drop off the bone.

SERVES 4

Preheat the oven to 160 °C. Brown the shanks on both sides in the heated cooking oil in a heavy-based frying pan. Add the onions and the garlic and sauté. Season with the salt, pepper and seasoning salt.

Transfer the mixture to a casserole dish and add the heated meat stock and wine. Place the lid on top of the casserole dish and roast for 3–4 hours or until the meat is tender.

Just prior to serving, stir in the orange juice and orange rind. Sprinkle with the chopped parsley and shredded peel and serve with mangetout and basmati rice.

4 lamb shanks (ask your butcher to saw through the bone in two equal places down the shank bone)
100 ml cooking oil
2 onions, chopped
2 cloves garlic, crushed
5 ml salt
2.5 ml freshly ground black pepper
5 ml seasoning salt
500 ml hot meat stock
200 ml dry white wine
juice of 4 oranges and the rind of 2 oranges
250 ml chopped fresh parsley
shredded orange peel to garnish

crème *Caramel*

*This dessert is as smooth as silk and Leon always teases me and says:
'Faygie, this is no good – I found a single bubble!'*

MAKES 1 LARGE OR 6 SMALL

To make the caramel:
Pour the sugar and water into a heavy-based saucepan. Melt over high heat, stirring constantly. Add the cream of tartar. The sugar will slowly begin to change colour. When golden brown, pour the caramel carefully to coat the base of either a non-stick 1 kg loaf pan or single-serving porcelain or aluminium moulds. Set the mould(s) aside to cool.

To make the custard:
Preheat the oven to 180 °C. Whisk the eggs and yolk, and sugar and vanilla until blended.

Scald the milk in a heavy-based saucepan, then pour it very slowly into the egg mixture, beating continuously.

Pour the custard over the caramel-coated mould(s) and place in a large baking tin, half filled with hot, not boiling water. Bake at 180 °C for 30 minutes, then reduce the oven temperature to 160 °C for 1 hour or until set.

Remove from the oven and, when cool, refrigerate to chill.

To serve:
To unmould the dessert, run a sharp knife around the edges of the mould(s). Dip the base(s) briefly into boiling water. Place a serving platter on top of the caramel and grasping both sides firmly, flip over.

The clever cook can linethe baking tin with a treble thickness of newspaper before pouring in the water. This acts as an insulator and prevents the custard from curdling. Cover the caramel with baking paper to prevent a skin from forming on top of the custard.

Caramel
200 g white sugar
60 ml boiling water
2 large pinches cream of tartar

Custard
3 jumbo eggs and 1 yolk
30 ml white sugar
5 ml vanilla essence
750 ml milk

Carmen's favourite *Chocolate Soufflé*

SERVES 4

Preheat the oven to 190 °C. Grease 4 x 250 ml ramekins with butter. Coat with the 15 ml castor sugar and shake out the excess. Place the ramekins on a baking tray.

Melt the butter in a heavy-based saucepan and add the flour and cocoa. Cook, stirring continuously, for 1 minute. Remove the saucepan from the heat and gradually whisk in the milk, stirring continuously over medium heat until the mixture boils and thickens.

Remove the saucepan from the heat and add the 100 ml castor sugar and stir until the sugar has dissolved. Transfer the mixture to a bowl.

Melt the chocolate in a heat-proof bowl over a saucepan of simmering water and stir into the milk mixture. Add the egg yolks and mix until combined. Using an electric beater, whisk the egg whites to soft peak stage. Stir the egg whites into the chocolate mixture using a metal spoon until combined.

Divide the mixture among the prepared ramekins and smooth the tops. Bake for 18–20 minutes or until puffed. Dust with icing sugar and serve immediately topped with a sprig of mint. If you prefer your soufflé 'runny', reduce the baking time to 15 minutes.

The clever cook can melt the chocolate in the microwave on 50 per cent power for 4 minutes. Allow to cool before adding it to the milk mixture.

50 g soft butter and extra for greasing
15 ml castor sugar for dusting
30 ml cake flour
15 ml cocoa powder
125 ml milk
100 ml castor sugar
100 g dark chocolate, chopped
4 jumbo eggs, separated
icing sugar for dusting
sprigs of mint to decorate

My youngest daughter Carmen, like her mother, is a total chocoholic!

She first 'discovered' the flavour of high-quality chocolate on one of

our many vacations in the south of France.

my roasted Tomato Soup

SERVES 4

To make the soup:
Preheat the oven to 220 °C. Pour the olive oil into a roasting pan and heat in the oven until almost smoking. Carefully tip in the plum tomatoes, onion rings and garlic, and toss to coat in the oil. Scatter over the thyme and basil and sprinkle with the sugar. Season generously with the salt and pepper. Roast in the oven for 40–45 minutes, stirring once or twice until caramelized.

Tip the roasted tomatoes and flavourings into a heavy-based saucepan and add the soup, orange juice and rind. Bring to the boil, and cook for 5 minutes. Place the tomato mixture into a food processor fitted with a metal blade and process until smooth and creamy in texture. Taste and adjust the seasoning. If using, stir in the cream or milk and reheat.

To make the garnish:
Heat the olive oil in a heavy-based frying pan. Snip the vine tomatoes into four clusters and fry them on the vine for about 1 minute. Pour the soup into warmed bowls and top with the pan-roasted vine tomatoes. Drizzle the pan juices around the tomatoes and scatter with basil leaves.

The clever cook can cut a couple of corners and omit the plum tomatoes and the onions – this will result in a smoother textured soup. I often prepare this version when my children have a host of friends on a winter's evening.

100 ml olive oil
1 kg plum tomatoes, halved
2 onions, thinly sliced
  into rings
2 cloves garlic, halved
50 ml chopped fresh thyme
50 ml chopped fresh basil
30 ml castor sugar
salt and freshly ground
  black pepper
3 x 410 g cans tomato soup
juice and rind of 1 orange
250 ml fresh cream or milk
  (optional) (I always add
  cream)

Garnish
30 ml olive oil
250 g baby cherry tomatoes on
  the vine
small fresh basil leaves

Your guests will love this soup and won't believe that it only took a couple of minutes to prepare. The soup is delicious with or without the cream or milk. If you like a tart-flavoured soup, omit the cream or milk.

Quail Egg, Avocado and Asparagus *platter*

This combination of quail eggs, avocado and green asparagus is a firm favourite of my family. I serve this as a side dish for a casual supper and it works as successfully for a formal buffet supper. I leave the peeling of the eggs to Tamara or Carmen – this is not the most pleasant task.

SERVES 6

Boil the quail eggs in a saucepan of water for 5 minutes. Pour off the water and peel the eggs immediately under cold running water. Halve and set aside.

Trim off the ends of the asparagus and drop into a heavy-based saucepan of boiling water. Add the salt and sugar. Boil the asparagus for 3 minutes until slightly crisp. Drain and refresh in cold water. Set aside.

Halve the avocados, remove the stones and slice lengthways. Drizzle with lemon juice to prevent discoloration. Set aside.

Arrange the quail eggs, asparagus and avocado on a serving platter and garnish with the lemon slices and fresh herbs.

The clever cook can add 125 ml tarragon vinegar to the herbed mayonnaise (page 79) and serve on the side as a dressing for the salad.

24 quail eggs
500 g washed fresh
    green asparagus
5 ml salt
10 ml white sugar
4 ripe avocados
50 ml lemon juice
lemon slices
fresh herbs

Warm Salad of Root Vegetables
with horseradish dressing

This dish also works as an accompaniment to the salmon, roast beef or rack of lamb.

SERVES 4

To make the salad:

Preheat the oven to 190 °C. Wrap the beetroot in aluminium foil and place alongside the potatoes, turnips, carrots, onions and garlic in a large roasting pan. Drizzle the vegetables with the olive oil and season to taste with the salt and pepper. Bake for 1 hour or until tender. Cool the vegetables slightly, then peel the beetroot. Cut the beetroot in half and arrange on a serving platter together with the remaining vegetables.

To make the dressing:

Combine the garlic, horseradish cream and mustard in a small bowl. Whisk in the vinegar and olive oil and season to taste with the salt and pepper.

To serve:

Drizzle the dressing over the vegetables and garnish with watercress. Serve warm with crusty bread.

500 g baby beetroot, scrubbed and trimmed

450 g baby potatoes, scrubbed and halved

2 turnips, trimmed, peeled and cut into 1 cm thick slices

400 g baby carrots, trimmed and peeled

12 peeled baby onions

1 bulb garlic, cloves separated

100 ml olive oil

sea salt and freshly ground black pepper

watercress to garnish and crusty bread for serving

Horseradish dressing

1 clove garlic, crushed

30 ml horseradish cream

5 ml wholegrain mustard

15 ml red wine vinegar

100 ml extra virgin olive oil

sea salt and freshly ground black pepper

Grilled Tuna Salad *with citrus and olive vinaigrette*

I love the flavour of rare tuna. This recipe works equally well with fresh swordfish, but remember that it needs to be cooked for a little longer. This salad is also delicious served with wasabi mayonnaise (page 196) instead of vinaigrette.

SERVES 6

To prepare the tuna:

Combine the olive oil, lemon juice and salt and pepper in a small bowl and stir until blended. Place the tuna in a zip-lock plastic bag and pour in the marinade. Turn the tuna to coat evenly. Close the bag and refrigerate for between 30 minutes and up to 2 hours.

Heat a heavy-based grilling pan and grill the tuna for 3–4 minutes on each side for rare or until the required degree of doneness.

To make the vinaigrette:

Combine all the ingredients in a medium-size bowl. Taste and adjust the seasoning. Set aside.

To serve:

Divide the spinach among the serving plates and arrange the tuna on top. Spoon some vinaigrette over and serve immediately.

The clever cook can prepare the vinaigrette up to 6 hours ahead, cover and refrigerate. Remove the vinaigrette from the refrigerator 30 minutes prior to serving.

30 ml extra virgin olive oil
30 ml fresh lemon juice
salt and freshly ground
    black pepper
500 g centre-cut tuna fillets,
    about 2.5 cm thick
200 g fresh baby spinach leaves

Vinaigrette

100 ml extra virgin olive oil
15 ml fresh lemon juice
juice of 1 orange
1 onion, chopped
1 orange, peeled, sectioned and
    coarsely chopped
20 black olives
30 ml rinsed capers
30 ml chopped fresh parsley
salt and freshly ground
    black pepper

Tamara's Favourite Fettuccine
with smoked salmon and caviar

SERVES 6

Cook the pasta in a saucepan of salted boiling water until just tender. Drain and set aside.

Heat the olive oil in a large heavy-based frying pan and sauté the onions until tender. Add the pasta, vodka, fresh and sour creams, and toss lightly.

Just prior to serving, stir in both caviars and add pepper to taste. Spoon onto a serving platter, sprinkle with the chives and top with the smoked salmon. Serve hot.

The clever cook can boil the pasta in advance, rinse under cold running water and sprinkle with olive oil or cooking oil to prevent it from coagulating.

500 g fettuccine
50 ml olive oil
2 red onions, chopped
50 ml vodka
250 ml fresh cream
250 ml sour cream
100 g black caviar
100 g red caviar
freshly ground black pepper
50 ml snipped fresh chives
250 g smoked salmon,
    cut into strips

This is my daughter Tamara's favourite dish,
as she loves the delicate flavour combination.
No doubt the vodka in this recipe
adds an extra zing to this dish!

fruity Chicken Breasts

Most of the guests I entertain prefer chicken breasts to the brown meat of the chicken.
This dish is delicious and an excellent recipe for the calorie-conscious guest!

SERVES 4

Combine the cooking oil, lemon juice, brandy, brown sugar and soy sauce in a plastic container and marinate the chicken breasts for 2–3 hours in the refrigerator.

Preheat the oven to 180 °C. Remove the chicken breasts from the marinade and place in an ovenproof casserole dish coated with cooking spray, or greased with butter or vegetable fat, and bake for 40–60 minutes while basting frequently with the remaining marinade.

Add the peaches and apricots and bake for an additional 15 minutes or until the fruit is tender. Garnish with wild rocket and serve with basmati rice and Oriental Vegetables in Coconut Cream (page 85).

The clever cook can barbecue the chicken over moderate coals for about 40 minutes, basting frequently with the marinade.

The fruit should still be baked in the oven. I have also used canned peaches and apricots when the fresh option is out of season.

125 ml cooking oil
50 ml fresh lemon juice
50 ml brandy
30 ml brown sugar
10 ml soy sauce
8 skinless chicken breast fillets
6 ripe peaches, peeled, split
    and stoned
6 ripe apricots, split and stoned
wild rocket to garnish

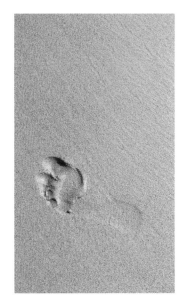

oven-roasted *American Porterhouse Steak*

An American porterhouse steak with its T-shaped bone is cut 5 cm thick from the sirloin section closest to the rump. This thick steak serves two persons and is cut against the grain, serving the sirloin and fillet separately. Each guest is served with a portion of both muscles.

SERVES 2

Preheat the oven to 180 °C. Slash the fat at the edges around the steak at 2.5 cm intervals to prevent curling during the roasting process. Season the meat with the salt, pepper and olive oil. Combine all the basting ingredients in a bowl and set aside.

Place the meat on the rack of an oven-roasting pan and roast for:
Rare: 15–20 minutes per 500 g plus 20 minutes extra.
Medium: 20–25 minutes per 500 g plus 25 minutes extra. Baste the meat frequently during the roasting process. To carve, first remove the bone and discard it, then carve thin slices of both the sirloin and fillet sections by cutting across the width of the steak. Serve with roasted potato wedges and a green salad.

1 American porterhouse steak (T-bone), 5 cm thick
5 ml salt
2.5 ml freshly ground black pepper
50 ml olive oil

Basting mixture
50 ml dry white wine
50 ml fresh lemon juice
50 ml cooking oil
2 cloves garlic, crushed
5 ml salt
2.5 ml freshly ground black pepper
2 sprigs of fresh thyme
10 ml grated lemon rind

Sam's Favourite Lamb Chops *and mint jelly*

SERVES 4

To make the mint jelly:
Bring the apple juice to the boil in a small heavy-based saucepan. Place the mint leaves in a small bowl and pour the apple juice over. Allow to infuse for 20 minutes, then strain. Add the vinegar and sugar to the strained liquid. Heat to dissolve the sugar. DO NOT BOIL. Remove from the heat and add the gelatine. Stir until the gelatine dissolves. Pour into warm, sterilized jars. Cool and seal.

To prepare the lamb chops:
Slash the fat at the edges of the chops. Season the chops with the salt, pepper, rosemary, garlic and olive oil.

Grill in a heated grilling pan for 5–7 minutes per side or until required degree of doneness and until the chops are brown on both sides. Use tongs to turn the meat. Pour off any excess fat that accumulates in the pan. Serve immediately with the mint jelly.

The clever cook can place the cooked chops in an open ovenproof dish at 100 °C to crisp until ready to serve.

8 lamb rib chops, 2.5 cm thick
5 ml salt
2.5 ml freshly ground
   black pepper
15 ml chopped fresh rosemary
2 cloves garlic, crushed
50 ml olive oil

Mint jelly
500 ml apple juice
100 ml fresh mint leaves,
   finely shredded
20 ml white vinegar
100 ml white sugar
20 ml gelatine powder softened
   in 50 ml cold water

I have named these chops after a good family friend, Sam Hackner. Sam has a healthy appetite and normally only prefers a single course meal and calls it a day after the starters. But when I invite the Hackners for a meal Sam will only accept the invitation if there are lamb chops on the menu, and then he always eats the main course!

Mango *sorbet*

This recipe (photograph left) is easy to prepare and far nicer than any bought variety.

MAKES 2.5 LITRES

Dissolve the sugar in the water in a heavy-based saucepan over high heat until the mixture reaches a syrupy consistency. Set aside. Add the mango purée.

Freeze for about 1 hour, then churn for 30 minutes until smooth in an ice-cream maker or in a food processor fitted with a metal blade.

700 g white sugar
500 ml water
2 litres mango purée

Lemon *sorbet*

MAKES 2 LITRES

Bring the sugar and the milk to the boil in a heavy-based saucepan. Stir until the sugar has dissolved. Add the lemon juice and rind.

Freeze for about 1 hour, then churn for 30 minutes until smooth in an ice-cream maker or in a food processor fitted with a metal blade.

500 g white sugar
1 litre milk
1 litre lemon juice
rind of 4 lemons

This sorbet (photograph left) is tart and delicious

to serve as a summer dessert or as a palate cleanser

between courses of a formal dinner party.

glacé *Zabaglione*

This dessert is the perfect finish to a summer lunch. Men often don't enjoy a dessert, but this one they love as it is light and smooth and has a subtle alcohol flavour.

SERVES 4

Prepare a double boiler. Whisk together the egg yolks and the sugar in the top of the double boiler using a balloon whisk. Add the Marsala. Whisk over low heat until very thick. The mixture should leave a trail on top.

Soak the gelatine in the water for 5 minutes. Dissolve over low heat or in a microwave on the defrost setting and allow to cool. Whisk the dissolved gelatine into the zabaglione. Place the top of the double boiler into a large bowl containing ice cubes. Stir gently until the mixture begins to set. Whip the cream until it begins to hold its shape. Fold the cream into the zabaglione mixture, then pour into chilled glasses. Leave to set in the refrigerator for about 1 hour.

Prior to serving, sprinkle with the almonds. Serve with Italian finger biscuits on the side.

4 large egg yolks
60 g castor sugar
75 ml Marsala or sweet sherry
5 ml gelatine powder
30 ml cold water
200 ml fresh cream
30 ml toasted flaked almonds
Italian finger biscuits
   for serving

Afternoon tea

AT MY TABLE

For a summer-time treat

paint a table top in candy stripes, set it out in a lush

garden with a soft breeze wafting through the willows

and bring out the fine china. Serve sweet treats like

Chocolate Cake and Custard Kisses, and finish off the

look by hanging clusters of roses in soft pastels and

pinks from overhanging branches.

most delicious Asparagus Quiche

This quiche is delicious served as a savoury for a winter afternoon's tea. The flan ring lined with the pastry may be prepared well ahead of time and chilled. A cold quiche is good picnic fare or makes a quick and satisfying snack.

SERVES 8

To make the pastry:

Preheat the oven to 220 °C. Sift the flour, salt, cayenne pepper and mustard powder together in a bowl. Rub the butter into the flour mixture and add the cheese. Add the egg yolk and cold water and combine to form a pliable dough. Wrap the dough in clingfilm and chill in the refrigerator for 20 minutes.

Coat a flan ring (25 cm diameter) or rectangular flan pan with cooking spray, or grease with butter or vegetable fat. Press in the cheese pastry to line the base and sides. Bake blind for 10–15 minutes.

To make the filling:

Reduce the oven temperature to 180 °C. Sauté the onions in the heated cooking oil in a heavy-based frying pan, then set aside.

Beat the eggs, cream, milk, cayenne pepper and salt together in a bowl. Sprinkle the cheeses and asparagus cuts over the baked pastry shell. Top with the onion and the asparagus spears. Pour the egg mixture over and bake for about 30 minutes or until the egg mixture is set.

Cheese Pastry

250 g cake flour

a pinch of salt

a pinch of cayenne pepper

a pinch of mustard powder

150 g butter

250 ml grated cheddar cheese

1 jumbo egg yolk

70 ml cold water

Filling

2 onions, chopped

30 ml cooking oil

2 jumbo eggs

125 ml fresh cream

125 ml milk

a pinch of cayenne pepper

2.5 ml salt

250 ml grated cheddar cheese

250 ml grated gruyère or
   mozzarella cheese

1 x 450 g can asparagus cuts,
   drained

1 x 450 g can asparagus spears,
   drained

the best Chocolate Cake

Chocolate cake is a South African favourite. This version is as light as a typical chiffon cake and the chocolate glaze adds the finishing touch.

SERVES 10–12

To make the cake:
Preheat the oven to 180 °C. Dissolve the cocoa in the boiling water, cool and set aside. Sift the flour, baking powder and 250 ml castor sugar into the bowl of an electric mixer. Make a well in the centre and add the oil, egg yolks, cocoa mixture and vanilla and beat thoroughly.

In a separate bowl beat the egg whites and salt until stiff peak stage. Add the remaining 50 ml castor sugar to the egg whites and beat for 1 minute. Fold the chocolate mixture into the egg white mixture.

Pour the mixture into an ungreased chiffon pan (tube pan) and bake for 55–60 minutes. When the cake is cooked, invert the pan onto a bottle and leave suspended until cool. Loosen the edges of the cake with a knife and remove from the pan.

To make the icing:
Cream the butter, icing sugar and cocoa together in an electric mixer. Add the eggs, one at a time, followed by the vanilla essence. Beat until smooth.

To make the chocolate glaze:
Melt the chocolate in the water in a double boiler. Add the milk or cream and the butter and combine until smooth.

Ice the sides and top of the cake, then drizzle the chocolate glaze over the cake, allowing it to run down the sides.

50 ml cocoa powder
150 ml boiling water
375 ml cake flour
15 ml baking powder
300 ml castor sugar
200 ml cooking oil
7 egg yolks
10 ml vanilla essence
8 egg whites
a pinch of salt

Icing
160 g soft butter
500 ml icing sugar
200 ml cocoa powder
3 jumbo eggs
2.5 ml vanilla essence

Chocolate glaze
200 g dark chocolate
50 ml water
50 ml milk or fresh cream
50 g butter

chocolate Marie Biscuit Fingers

MAKES 30

300 g butter, softened

800 g icing sugar

2 jumbo eggs, beaten

60 ml cocoa powder

a pinch of salt

2 x 200 g packets Marie
biscuits, broken into pieces

10 ml vanilla essence

Melt the butter in a heavy-based saucepan but do not allow it to boil. Add the icing sugar, eggs, cocoa powder and salt. Mix thoroughly. Add the biscuits and vanilla essence.

Coat a lamington pan with cooking spray and press the biscuit mixture into the pan. Cool. Cut into fingers.

The clever cook can add 100 g glacé cherries for a fruity flavour.

Custard *kisses*

MAKES 35–40

To make the biscuits:
Preheat the oven to 200 °C. Cream the butter and sugar together in an electric mixer until creamy. Add the eggs, one at a time, beating after each addition.

Sift together the flour, custard powder and baking powder and spoon into the sugar mixture.

Mix until thoroughly combined. Grease a baking tray and drop teaspoonfuls of the dough onto the tray. Bake for 8 minutes.

To make the icing:
Place the butter in the bowl of an electric mixer and beat until smooth and as white as possible. Gradually add half the icing sugar, beating continuously. Add the remaining icing sugar and, if necessary, the milk. The icing should be smooth and easy to spread with a spatula.

To assemble:
Sandwich the biscuit halves together with the butter icing.

250 g butter
250 ml white sugar
4 jumbo eggs
500 ml cake flour
250 g custard powder
10 ml baking powder

Butter icing
125 g butter, at room temperature
375 ml icing sugar
15 ml milk (optional)

four layer Apple Tart

This apple tart is the nicest I have eaten. I have also served it successfully as a dessert.

MAKES 10 SLICES OR 6 INDIVIDUAL SERVINGS

To make the pastry:

Preheat the oven to 200 °C. Beat the butter and sugar together in an electric mixer until smooth and creamy. Add the vanilla and the eggs. Sift the flour and salt together.

With the mixer on its lowest speed add the flour in three or four stages. As soon as the mixture comes together as a crumbly dough, stop the machine. Gather the dough together and turn out onto a lightly floured surface. Briefly knead the pastry with your hands until smooth. Wrap the pastry in clingfilm and place in the refrigerator for 30 minutes.

Coat a 21 cm loose-base round or rectangular flan pan (or 6 single-serving, 13 cm quiche pans) with cooking spray, or grease with butter or vegetable fat. Roll out the pastry to 3 mm thick and line the base and sides of the flan pan. Refrigerate for 20 minutes. Bake blind for 15 minutes, then set aside.

To make the filling:

Cut the apples into cubes. Heat the butter in a large heavy-based pan until sizzling. Sauté the apples for 5–7 minutes or until golden brown and slightly softened. Add the Calvados and cook until all the liquid has evaporated. Set aside to cool.

Spoon the apples into the pastry base and scatter over the sultanas and raspberries.

To make the streusel topping:

Reduce the oven temperature to 180 °C. Sift the flour with the cinnamon into a bowl. Rub in the butter until the mixture resembles fine breadcrumbs. Stir in the sugar and the crushed biscuits. Sprinkle the topping over the fruit. Bake the tart(s) for 20–30 minutes or until the topping is crisp and golden. Place the flan pan on a cooling rack and leave to cool.

To serve:

To unmould the tart, press up the base of the pan and slide the tart onto a large plate. Serve warm with whipped cream on the side.

The clever cook can wrap any of the leftover pastry in clingfilm and freeze for later use. This tart is quite crumbly so to make slicing easier use a long-bladed hot knife. Simply dip the knife in a jug of boiling water, dry and use immediately.

Pastry

250 g butter, softened
180 g castor sugar
5 ml vanilla essence
2 jumbo eggs, beaten
500 g cake flour
2.5 ml salt

Filling

5 large Granny Smith or
    Golden Delicious apples,
    peeled, cored and quartered
50 g butter
50 ml Calvados (apple brandy)
100 g sultanas
200 g raspberries

Streusel topping

100 g cake flour
2.5 ml ground cinnamon
60 g butter
80 g brown sugar
8 digestive biscuits,
    finely crushed

Ginger Cake *with glazed ginger whip*

Ginger cake is a lovely old favourite – this cake is easy to prepare and keeps well, and is immensely popular with all members of my family.

SERVES 10–12

To make the cake:

Preheat the oven to 180 °C. Beat the eggs and sugar together in an electric mixer until creamy. Add the oil and syrup. Sift the flour, ginger, cinnamon, allspice and salt together in a mixing bowl, then add it to the creamed mixture. Add the tea followed by the baking powder and bicarbonate of soda. Pour the cake mixture into a greased and floured fluted pan and bake for 50 minutes or until a knife inserted in the centre comes out clean. Unmould and leave to cool.

To make the ginger whip:

Beat the cream until it begins to hold its shape. Stir in the chopped glazed ginger and the ginger syrup. Refrigerate. Serve a dollop of the ginger whip on the side of each slice of cake.

2 jumbo eggs

125 ml white sugar

250 ml cooking oil

250 ml golden syrup

500 ml cake flour

10 ml ground ginger

5 ml ground cinnamon

5 ml ground allspice

2.5 ml salt

250 ml strong black tea, cooled

5 ml baking powder

10 ml bicarbonate of soda

Glazed ginger whip

250 ml fresh cream

125 ml chopped glazed ginger

15 ml ginger syrup

ma's *Fruit Ring Cake*

*This cake is pure heaven! It has the rich flavour of a fruit cake,
but is more moist and much lighter.*

SERVES 10–12

160 g butter
250 ml white sugar
2 jumbo eggs
5 ml bicarbonate of soda
200 ml milk
500 ml cake flour
a pinch of salt
250 ml chopped dates
125 ml chopped mixed nuts
125 ml chopped glacé cherries
30 ml chopped dried citrus peel
orange zest to decorate

Syrup
250 ml fresh orange juice
grated rind of 2 oranges
125 ml white sugar

To make the cake:
Preheat the oven to 180 °C.
Cream the butter and sugar in
an electric mixer until smooth
and creamy. Add the eggs and
mix thoroughly. Dissolve the
bicarbonate of soda in the milk.
Sift the flour and salt together
in a bowl and add to the
creamed mixture alternately
with the milk mixture. Add the
dates, nuts, cherries and citrus
peel and mix until combined.
   Spoon the mixture into a
greased and floured bundt pan
(tube pan) and bake for 1 hour.

To make the syrup:
Combine the orange juice,
orange rind and sugar in a small
heavy-based saucepan and bring
to the boil. Set aside to cool.

To assemble:
Unmould the cake as soon as it
comes out of the oven and pour
the syrup over. Top with orange
zest to decorate.

Orange Chocolate *squares*

These chocolate squares are great for children's birthday parties.

MAKES 24

To make the chocolate squares:
Preheat the oven to 180 °C.
Place all the ingredients, except
your chosen decoration, into
the bowl of an electric mixer
and beat until combined.

Grease and flour a lamington
pan lined with baking paper.
Pour the cake mixture into the
pan and bake for 25–30 minutes.
Turn the cake out onto a cooling
rack, remove the paper and set
aside to cool.

To make the icing:
Cream the butter until soft
using an electric beater. Add the
egg yolk, salt, grated rind and
orange juice. Blend in the icing
sugar until the icing is smooth
and of a spreading consistency.

To serve:
Ice the cake with the
orange butter icing and cut
it into squares. Decorate
with orange zest, chocolate
vermicelli or Smarties®.

125 g butter, softened
200 ml white sugar
375 ml cake flour
10 ml baking powder
200 ml milk
30 ml cocoa powder
2.5 ml salt
5 ml vanilla essence
2 jumbo eggs
orange zest, chocolate or
    Smarties® to decorate

Orange butter icing
100 g butter
1 jumbo egg yolk
a pinch of salt
grated rind and juice of
    1 orange
450 g icing sugar

a splendid *Plum or Apricot Tart*

This recipe is so easy to prepare and the almond cream perfectly complements the tartness of the fruit.

SERVES 8

To make the pastry:
Cream the butter and sugar in a food processor fitted with a plastic blade. Add the egg and combine. Add the flour and salt and process until the dough forms a ball. Wrap the dough in clingfilm and refrigerate for 2 hours.

To make the almond cream:
Cream the butter and sugar together until light and fluffy in a food processor fitted with a plastic blade. Add the eggs and combine. Combine the almonds with the cake flour and add to the mixture. Add the almond essence and process for a few seconds. Set aside.

To assemble:
Preheat the oven to 190 °C. Coat a 23 cm loose-base flan pan with cooking spray, or grease with butter or vegetable fat, and press in the pastry to line the base and sides.

Spoon in the almond cream. Arrange the plums or apricots in concentric circles, cut side up, until the whole surface is covered with fruit. Sprinkle the fruit with the sugar and dot with butter. Bake for 45 minutes or until cooked. Serve with whipped cream or crème fraîche on the side.

The clever cook can make individual mini tarts and use a combination of plums and apricots as a variation.

10–12 fresh ripe plums or
apricots, halved and stoned
50 ml white sugar
50 g butter
whipped cream or crème
fraîche for serving

Pastry
250 g unsalted butter
250 g castor sugar
1 jumbo egg
500 g cake flour
2.5 ml salt

Almond cream
250 g butter
250 g castor sugar
4 jumbo eggs, beaten
250 g ground almonds
60 g cake flour
2.5 ml almond essence

Carrot *cake*

SERVES 10–12

To make the cake:

Preheat the oven to 190 °C. Beat together the sugar and oil in the bowl of an electric mixer for 2–3 minutes. Add the eggs and beat thoroughly.

Sift the flour, baking powder, bicarbonate of soda, cinnamon and ginger together in a bowl and add to the sugar mixture together with the carrots, nuts, sultanas and pineapple. Mix until combined.

Pour the mixture into a greased and floured 23 cm bundt pan (tube pan) or a 25 cm round cake pan and bake for 50–60 minutes or until cooked when tested with a skewer. Set aside to cool in the tin

This carrot cake has a delicate tropical flavour. The pineapple not only enhances the flavour but ensures the cake is deliciously moist.

To make the icing:

Cream the butter in the bowl of an electric mixer and add the icing sugar and vanilla. Add the cream cheese, lemon juice and lemon rind and combine until smooth. Do not overbeat as the icing will become too watery.

To assemble:

Once the cake has cooled, turn it out and spread the top and sides with the cream cheese icing. Sprinkle the top with chopped pecan nuts.

250 ml brown sugar

200 ml cooking oil

4 jumbo eggs

375 ml cake flour

10 ml baking powder

5 ml bicarbonate of soda

5 ml ground cinnamon

2.5 ml ground ginger

500 ml grated carrots

125 ml chopped pecan nuts

125 ml sultanas

250 ml canned crushed
   pineapple, drained or
   250 ml apple sauce

50 g pecan nuts, chopped

Cream cheese icing

120 g butter

500 g icing sugar

5 ml vanilla essence

250 g smooth cream cheese

15 ml fresh lemon juice

5 ml grated lemon rind

Biltong *bites*

SERVES 8

To make the pastry:
Preheat the oven to 190 °C.
Sift the flour, salt and cayenne
pepper together in a bowl and
rub in the butter. Add the
cheese, egg yolks and lemon
juice. Knead to form a dough.

Roll out the dough on a
lightly floured surface to 6 mm
thick and cut with a small scone
cutter or any fancy biscuit
cutter. Place on an ungreased
baking tray and bake for
10 minutes. Allow to cool.

To make the biltong butter:
Mix together the butter,
biltong and lemon juice until
well combined.

To assemble:
Sandwich the pastry sections
together with the biltong butter.

The clever cook can sandwich
the shapes together with a
spread of smooth apricot jam
or with a combination of butter
and vegetable extract, such
as Marmite®.

250 g cake flour
2.5 ml salt
a pinch of cayenne pepper
250 g butter
250 g cheddar cheese, grated
2 jumbo egg yolks, beaten
15 ml fresh lemon juice

Biltong butter
100 g butter, melted
50 g biltong, grated
10 ml fresh lemon juice

These light, cheesy pastries are a hit every time I serve them. They are also very versatile
and can be served as a light afternoon snack or as a nibble with early evening cocktails.

Snacks
AT MY TABLE

With a sunset deck and gently lapping rock pools,

not much else is required to create the perfect setting

for evening snacks. Wrap the trees in fairy lights and

strings rows of white chrysanthemums, lanterns and

hanging decorations between the branches. Tulips

casually placed in square glass vases and tea lights

add an extra sparkle. Decorate the cocktail umbrellas

with silver rhinestones and sequins.

Anchovy Straws with lemon mayonnaise

If you have never baked with quick puff pastry before, this recipe is a great place to start.
Serve the anchovy straws as an hors d'oeuvre, or with salads or soups.

SERVES 10

To make the pastry:

Sift the flour and salt into a bowl twice. Cut the butter into the flour and rub in lightly with your fingertips. Combine the lemon juice and egg yolk. Add it to the flour/butter mixture and combine to form a stiff pastry. Cover with clingfilm and leave to chill in the refrigerator for about 1 hour.

Lightly flour the work surface and roll out the pastry into a rectangle, 3 mm thick. Halve the rectangle lengthways, wrap one half in clingfilm and keep in the refrigerator.

If the anchovies are too thick, halve them lengthways. Starting 15 mm in from the edge of the pastry lay a line of anchovies along the length of the rectangle. Repeat to make three more lines, leaving a 20 mm space between each one. Brush the exposed pastry between the anchovies with the egg wash.

Take the other piece of pastry from the refrigerator, lift it on the rolling pin and lay it over the first pastry sheet. Press firmly with your fingertips to seal, taking care not to press down on the anchovies. Chill in the refrigerator for 20 minutes.

Trim and neaten the pastry edges. Cut the pastry rectangle widthwise into long strips, 20–30 mm wide. The pastry strips will be dotted with anchovy pieces. As you cut the anchovy straws, place them on a baking tray coated with cooking spray, flat-side down. Bake at 200 °C for 5–7 minutes. If the straws in the corners of the baking sheet are cooked before the rest, lift them off with a palette knife so that they do not burn. Cool on a wire rack.

To make the mayonnaise:

Place the egg yolks, lemon juice, lemon rind, salt and pepper in a food processor fitted with a plastic blade and whisk until combined. Add the oil, drop by drop, whisking constantly. When the mixture starts to thicken, add the remaining oil in a steady stream until fully incorporated. If the mayonnaise is too thick, dilute with 15 ml warm water.

The clever cook can refrigerate the mayonnaise for up to 5 days and the pastry, if well wrapped, will keep in the refrigerator for 2 days or in the freezer for 1 month.

Quick puff pastry

500 g cake flour
5 ml salt
500 g butter
30 ml fresh lemon juice
1 jumbo egg yolk
flour for dusting
1 x jar of 20 anchovy fillets
    in oil
1 jumbo egg yolk mixed with
    15 ml milk

Lemon mayonnaise

2 jumbo egg yolks
50 ml fresh lemon juice
rind of 1 lemon
salt and freshly ground
    black pepper
200 ml cooking oil

Coriander Chicken satay

SERVES 4

To make the satays:

Cut the chicken breast fillets into 3 cm cubes. Mix together the spices, garlic, sugar and salt and roll the chicken pieces in the mixture. Cover and refrigerate for at least 2 hours.

Preheat the barbecue or grill. Thread the chicken onto skewers. Cover the ends of the skewers with aluminium foil to prevent them burning. Brush the satays with oil. Place them onto the barbecue and grill for about 10 minutes or until cooked, turning frequently. Serve immediately with the peanut sauce.

To make the peanut sauce:

Fry the peanuts in the heated cooking oil until golden brown. Add the garlic, chillies and sugar. Place the mixture in a food processor fitted with a metal blade and process until fine in texture, then transfer to a small heavy-based saucepan.

Pour in the water and season with salt. Bring to the boil, then reduce the heat and simmer, stirring constantly for about 5 minutes. Stir in the coconut milk and transfer the sauce to a serving bowl. Serve on the side with the chicken satays.

The clever cook can soak wooden or bamboo skewers in water for at least 2 hours prior to using to prevent them burning.

750 g chicken breast fillets
15 ml ground coriander
15 ml turmeric
2 cloves garlic, crushed
45 ml white sugar
15 ml salt
cooking oil for basting

Peanut sauce
125 g raw peanuts
cooking oil for frying
2 cloves garlic, crushed
2 fresh red chillies, seeded
    and chopped
15 ml white sugar
375 ml water
salt to taste
250 ml coconut milk

Visitors to Malaysia and Singapore never forget the satay — grilled skewered meat, poultry or fish. Satay vendors are part of the charm of the city streets and the smell of the grilled food is irresistible.

Corn Fritters with selected toppings

SERVES 6–8

To make the corn fritters:
Combine the olive oil, egg yolks and water in a bowl and whisk until combined. Gradually add the flour to form a thick batter. Season with the salt and pepper. Stir in the corn kernels and onion. Whisk the egg whites until stiff peak stage, then fold them into the batter.

Heat 1 cm olive oil in a large heavy-based frying pan and fry tablespoonfuls of the mixture in batches for 2–3 minutes. Turn, using two spatulas, and cook for another 2–3 minutes until golden brown. Drain on paper towelling. Place in the oven at 125 °C to keep warm. Set out on platters just before serving.

Toppings:
Use any of the following as toppings for the fritters:
* Thinly sliced fried chicken livers, garnished with thinly sliced gherkin
* Roast beef and horseradish sauce, garnished with sprigs of fresh dill or parsley
* Sliced salami, garnished with radish or black olives
* Flaked snoek, garnished with slices of cucumber, black olives and sprigs of thyme
* Thinly sliced smoked salmon, garnished with chopped capers and a slice of lemon

Corn fritters

30 ml olive oil
2 jumbo eggs, separated
100 ml water
140 g cake flour
5 ml salt
a pinch of freshly ground black pepper
3 cobs of corn, kernels removed and reserved
1 onion, chopped
extra olive oil for frying

Well-prepared and perfectly fried fritters should be light, crisp and golden outside, soft and creamy inside and served soon after they have been cooked. Serve the fritters on their own as a snack or include a salad and turn this dish into a light lunch.

Grilled Mushrooms *with cheese and seafood topping*

SERVES 6

6 large brown mushrooms

30 ml olive oil

2 cloves garlic, crushed

30 ml chopped fresh parsley

30 ml butter

30 ml cake flour

250 ml milk

25 ml medium-cream sherry

300 g cooked marinara or
  seafood mix or a
  combination of white fish

15 ml fresh lemon juice

250 ml grated gruyère cheese

chopped fresh parsley to
  garnish

Preheat the oven to 180 °C. Wipe the mushrooms with paper towelling. Place the mushrooms, gills up, in a flat, greased casserole dish.

Heat the olive oil in a heavy-based frying pan and fry the garlic and parsley to release the flavour. Sprinkle this over the mushrooms. Melt the butter in a small heavy-based saucepan and add the flour and stir to form a paste. Add the milk and stir constantly until the sauce is smooth and has thickened. Stir in the sherry, seafood mix and lemon juice and bring to the boil. Spoon the seafood mix onto the mushrooms. Bake for 20 minutes. Remove the mushrooms from the oven and sprinkle the cheese on top, then return to the oven for an additional 5 minutes. Serve with a fork.

These mushrooms make a delicious weekend luncheon dish, served with a crisp salad.

Ladies on Horseback

MAKES 24

Marinate the livers in the red wine for 30 minutes. Cut each rasher of meat in half. Place a water chestnut and a piece of liver in the centre of the meat strip. Wrap the meat firmly around the filling and secure with a toothpick. Place under the preheated element of the oven grill and turn occasionally. Grill for 1–2 minutes or until cooked and golden brown.

250 g chicken livers, cleaned, trimmed and cut into pieces
250 g sliced pastrami, pickled brisket or maken rashers
100 ml dry red wine
1 x 230 g can water chestnuts, drained and halved

Although it is very much in vogue to serve small snacks with drinks in the lounge before a meal, few people realise that this custom is not as recent an innovation as is generally supposed. During their important feasts the ancient Greeks and Romans served snacks to their guests to stimulate their appetite. The European nations later developed the custom into something even more festive and attractive.

Savoury Cake with avocado, salmon and caviar

For a cocktail snack, I serve the larger version – almost like a pâté – with the oatcakes on the side. The single servings also works well as a starter for a buffet meal or as a savoury option for an afternoon tea. The oatcakes are a delicious accompaniment and will keep in a sealed container for a fortnight.

SERVES 8–10

Coat the base and sides of a 23 cm springform pan or single-serve moulds with cooking spray, or grease with butter or vegetable fat. Layer the smoked salmon around the sides and the base of the pan, covering the entire surface (if using single moulds, line the base only).

Combine the cream cheese and chives and spread it over the smoked salmon to form a second layer. Mash the avocado and combine it with the salt, cayenne pepper, lemon juice and half the mayonnaise. Spread this mixture over the cream cheese. Combine the salmon with the black pepper and remaining mayonnaise and spread the mixture on top of the layer of avocado. Top with the caviar and sprinkle the grated egg on top.

Refrigerate until ready to serve. Serve with crispbread, Melba toast or Oatcakes (see below) on the side.

200 g smoked salmon strips
3 x 250 g tubs smooth cream cheese
50 ml chopped fresh chives
4 ripe avocados, peeled
2.5 ml salt
a pinch of cayenne pepper
30 ml fresh lemon juice
100 ml mayonnaise
3 x 220 g cans pink salmon, drained and flaked
freshly ground black pepper
4 x 50 g jars black caviar
6 jumbo hard-boiled eggs, grated

Oatcakes

Preheat the oven to 190 °C. Sift the wholewheat and cake flours into a bowl. Add the oats and butter. Using your fingertips, rub in the butter until the mixture resembles breadcrumbs. Add the brown sugar and egg and mix to form a smooth dough.

Turn the dough onto a lightly floured surface and knead until smooth. Roll out until 3 mm thick, then cut into 5 cm rounds using a scone cutter. Place the oatcakes on a baking tray lined with baking paper. Bake for 20–25 minutes or until crisp. Leave to cool on a wire rack.

200 ml wholewheat flour
125 ml cake flour
200 ml oats
110 g soft butter
50 ml brown sugar
1 jumbo egg, beaten

Tartare of Scottish Salmon
with peppercorns and a lemon dressing

SERVES 6

To make the dressing:

Whisk the oil, mustard and lemon juice together in a small bowl and season to taste with the salt and pepper.

To make the salmon tartare:

Cut the salmon into 5 mm thick slices. Combine the salmon, onion, peppercorns and half the dressing in a small glass or ceramic bowl. Cover and refrigerate for 15–30 minutes to allow the flavours to develop. (Do not marinate for longer, as the lemon juice will cook the salmon.)

To make the croutons:

Preheat the oven to 100 °C. Cut the bread into 2–3 mm thick slices. Place the bread on baking trays and brush with the melted butter and sprinkle with the pepper. Bake for 5–20 minutes or until crisp but not coloured. Set aside.

To serve:

Place cucumber slices in a circle on each plate. Spoon the salmon tartare into the middle and sprinkle with the red and yellow peppers. Top with sour cream and sprinkle with dill. Spoon leftover dressing around the plates and sprinkle with salmon roe. Serve the croutons on the side.

Dressing

150 ml extra virgin olive oil
5 ml prepared hot mustard
15 ml fresh lemon juice
salt and freshly ground
    black pepper

Salmon tartare

600 g fresh, Scottish salmon,
    skin and bones removed
1 onion, finely chopped
15 g crushed black peppercorns

*Lemon pepper croutons
(optional)*

1 baguette
60 g butter, melted
5 ml lemon pepper

Cucumber salad

400 g English cucumber, cut
    into 5 mm thick slices
1 red pepper, seeded and
    finely chopped
1 yellow pepper, seeded and
    finely chopped
50 ml sour cream
15 ml chopped fresh dill
30 ml salmon roe

This versatile recipe can be served as canapés – one round

of cucumber topped with sliced salmon, sour cream, dill

and a crouton – or as a salad for a light summer lunch.

tomato and parmesan Puff Pastry Tarts

Ready-made pastry may be convenient, but nothing beats the home-made variety. As with most cooking, success in pastry-making comes from following a few simple rules and getting some practice.

SERVES 4

To make the pastry:

Place the 250 g flour, the salt and the butter (separately) in the freezer overnight.

Sift the flour and salt into a large bowl. Grate the butter and add half. Beat the egg, lemon juice and water together and stir the liquid into the flour mixture.

Turn out onto a board and roll into a 30 x 18 cm rectangle. Place the 60 g flour and cream of tartar in a sieve and sprinkle a little over the pastry. Scatter the remaining butter over half the pastry.

Fold the pastry in half to cover the butter. Roll out into a rectangle and fold into three. Lightly sprinkle both the board and the pastry with flour from the sieve. Give the pastry a 90 degree turn and continue to roll and fold six times, making sure that all the flour is used. Wrap the pastry in clingfilm and refrigerate for at least 1 hour.

Preheat the oven to 200 °C. Roll out the pastry to 5 mm thick. Cut out four rounds of 12 cm diameter using a saucer as a guide (you could also make smaller versions of about 6 cm diameter). Place the rounds on a baking tray and refrigerate for 20 minutes. Bake the pastry for 10 minutes, then place another baking tray on top to press the rounds down and keep them flat. Bake for a further 10 minutes until golden brown. Place on a cooling rack to cool and crisp.

To make the topping:

Arrange the tomato slices on a baking sheet in four overlapping circles the same size as the pastry rounds (if make the smaller versions, top with a single slice of tomato). Sprinkle with the balsamic vinegar, olive oil, basil and parsley. Place the parmesan

shavings on top. As the cheese melts it will hold the tomato slices together. Preheat the oven grill and place the tomatoes under the grill and watch carefully. The cheese does not need to brown but only melt to hold the tomato slices together. Remove the tomato slices from the oven.

To assemble:

Transfer each round of tomato onto a pastry round. Season the rocket with the olive oil, vinegar, salt and brown sugar. Pile on top of each tart and serve immediately.

Puff pastry

250 g cake flour

2.5 ml salt

250 g butter

1 jumbo egg

15 ml fresh lemon juice

90 ml cold water

60 g cake flour

5 ml cream of tarter

Tomato topping

8 ripe, plum tomatoes, skinned and sliced

30 ml balsamic vinegar

30 ml olive oil

15 ml chopped fresh basil

15 ml chopped fresh parsley

100 g parmesan cheese shavings

Salad

50 g rocket

30 ml extra virgin olive oil

15 ml balsamic vinegar

2.5 ml salt

5 ml brown sugar

Mini Potato Latkes *with avocado and smoked salmon*

Potato latkes are best served hot from the pan. Cooked latkes can be refrigerated for two days or successfully frozen for up to three months.

MAKES 20–24

To make the latkes:

Grate the potatoes and the onion in a food processor. Drain off the liquid. Add the salt, pepper and sugar. Add the beaten egg yolks, the flour and baking powder. Beat the egg whites until stiff, adding a pinch of salt, and fold into the mixture.

Drop spoonfuls of the mixture into 1 cm deep heated cooking oil in a deep frying pan to which a small piece of onion has been added. Fry the latkes on both sides for 3–4 minutes until golden brown. Drain the latkes on paper towelling and keep warm.

To make the topping:

Combine the avocados, lemon juice, salt and pepper. Spread a dollop of avocado onto each latke and top with the smoked salmon or biltong.

The clever cook folds in the stiffly beaten egg whites just before frying the latkes to ensure a crisp end result. You can reheat cooked frozen latkes by placing them on baking trays and heating at 220 °C for 6–7 minutes or until crisp to the touch and piping hot.

Latkes

3 large potatoes, peeled
1 onion
5 ml salt
a pinch of freshly ground
  black pepper
5 ml white sugar
2 jumbo eggs, separated
a pinch of salt
50 ml cake flour
5 ml baking powder
cooking oil for frying
small piece of onion

Topping

3 avocados, peeled, stoned
  and chopped
15 ml fresh lemon juice
2.5 ml salt
a pinch of freshly ground
  black pepper
slices of smoked salmon or
  shavings of biltong

Dinner
AT MY TABLE

Gazpacho

Rack of Lamb with Green Herb Crust

The Best Ever Chocolate mousse

Decked out in all its finery, this rich and opulent table combines deep oranges and golds, with a little Versace on the side.

Black velvet, burnt orange and copper roses arranged in low silver containers are offset with both tall and short single and multi-stemmed candelabra to create varying heights. Sugared oranges may be used as a base for place names, and printed menus add a little flair to the grand affair.

Gazpacho

No adjective can describe how easy this soup is to prepare or how delicious it tastes. I serve it as the first course of a formal dinner party or as a starter for a casual Sunday supper.

SERVES 8

Purée the canned tomatoes and the juice in a food processor fitted with a metal blade until smooth. Set aside. Blend the 250 ml tomato purée, garlic, cooking oil and bread until smooth, then add it to the puréed whole tomatoes. Add the lemon juice, lemon rind, sherry and brown sugar. Season to taste. I often need to add a little extra sugar and/or vinegar if the particular variety of canned tomato requires it.

The clever cook can serve croutons, chopped pickled cucumber and chopped red onion on the side. And, for a superb colour and taste sensation, combine this soup with the Chilled Courgette and Cucumber Soup (page 191) – pour both soups into the bowl simultaneously.

6 x 410 g cans whole peeled
   tomatoes
250 ml tomato purée
2 cloves garlic, crushed
250 ml cooking oil
8 slices fresh white bread,
   crusts removed
juice and rind of 2 lemons
100 ml sherry vinegar
50 ml brown sugar
salt and freshly ground
   black pepper

My Favourite Butternut Soup *with red pepper purée*

SERVES 6

To make the soup:

Heat the butter and olive oil in a heavy-based saucepan. Sauté the leeks until tender. Add the butternut and sweet potato, stirring frequently. Pour in the heated stock and herbs and simmer, covered, for about 20 minutes or until the vegetables are tender. Discard the herbs and purée the soup in a food processor fitted with a metal blade. Add the puréed soup to the sour cream and cream or milk and season to taste. Reheat.

To make the red pepper purée:

Place the peppers on the rack of a grilling pan about 10 cm from the element and grill until black and blistered. When cool, pull off the skin, starting at the stem end. Discard the stems, ribs and seeds. Purée the red pepper in a food processor fitted with a metal blade.

To serve:

Serve dollops of the roasted red pepper purée in the piping hot soup.

The clever cook can buy a jar of peppadews – whole, sweet piquant peppers – and drain and process these to serve with the soup instead of the red pepper purée.

50 g butter
50 ml olive oil
6 leeks, white part only,
    thinly sliced
2 kg butternut, peeled and
    diced
500 g sweet potatoes, peeled
    and diced
2 litres hot vegetable stock
a few sprigs of fresh thyme
a few sprigs of fresh parsley
125 ml sour cream
375 ml fresh cream or milk
salt and freshly ground
    black pepper
3 large sweet red peppers
flat-leaf parsley to garnish

I have eaten many a butternut soup in my lifetime and have found them to be either too thick, too thin or too flavoured with curry powder which, in my opinion, does nothing to enhance the taste. I prepare this soup at least once a week and any leftovers reheat successfully, needing only a slight dilution with some milk.

roasted *Asparagus Soup*

*This recipe combines the delicate flavour of fresh asparagus with the canned variety,
which is one of the most versatile and popular of all canned vegetables.*

SERVES 6

500 g fresh green
   asparagus tips, woody
   ends removed, rinsed
2 onions, sliced
50 ml olive oil
75 g butter
50 ml cake flour
500 ml milk
2 x 410 g cans asparagus cuts,
   drained and the liquid
   reserved
2 x 410 g cans asparagus soup
15 ml white sugar
salt and freshly ground
   black pepper
30 ml fresh lemon juice
250 ml fresh cream
50 ml fresh flat-leaf parsley

Preheat the oven to 180 °C.
Roast the asparagus tips and
the onions in the olive oil
in a roasting pan for about
30 minutes or until the
asparagus are tender. Remove
from the oven and purée the
asparagus and onions in a food
processor fitted with the metal
blade until smooth. Set aside.

Melt the butter in a heavy-
based saucepan and add the
cake flour. Stir until a smooth
paste forms. Add the milk
and stir continuously until
the mixture comes to the boil.
Slowly add the asparagus
cuts, liquid and canned soup.
Stir until thickened. Add the
puréed asparagus, sugar, salt,
pepper, lemon juice and cream.
Serve piping hot garnished
with the parsley.

The clever cook can sprinkle
grated cheddar cheese on top
prior to serving to add to the
nutritional value of the soup.

Chinese *Salad*

The interesting combination of the sweet and sour ingredients makes this salad ideal to serve with fish or poultry.

SERVES 4

Preheat the oven to 150 °C. Place the tomatoes on a baking tray, cut side up. Combine the vinegar, oil and brown sugar together and brush a little onto the tomatoes, reserving the remaining dressing. Season with the salt, pepper and garlic.

Roast for 20–25 minutes. Add the capers to the remaining dressing and drizzle over the roasted tomatoes. Arrange the rocket on a serving platter and scatter the tomatoes, avocado quarters and basil leaves over the rocket.

8 plum tomatoes, quartered
50 ml sherry vinegar
50 ml extra virgin olive oil
15 ml brown sugar
salt and freshly ground
    black pepper
1 clove garlic, crushed
30 ml capers, drained and
    crushed
50 g fresh rocket leaves
1 avocado, peeled and
    quartered
50 ml fresh basil leaves

Fish Terrine *with prawn sauce*

SERVES 6

To make the fish terrine:

Preheat the oven to 160 °C. Boil or poach the white fish in the milk in a heavy-based saucepan for 5 minutes or until cooked. Drain the fish and discard the milk, then flake the fish and set aside.

Sauté the leeks in the butter in a heavy-based saucepan. Add the flour and cook for 1 minute. Remove the saucepan from the heat and add the extra 250 ml milk while stirring constantly over low heat until thick and smooth. Add the anchovy sauce or chopped fillets and lemon juice.

Drain and flake the canned salmon, then place it and the fish in a food processor fitted with a metal blade. Process to a pulp. Pulse the egg yolks into the fish. Remove the fish mixture from the processor and add it to the sauce. Whisk the egg whites until stiff peak stage and fold into the fish mixture. Fold in the pepper.

Coat a loaf pan with cooking spray, or grease with butter or vegetable fat, and spoon the mixture into the pan. Cover the pan with a sheet of baking paper and bake for 50–60 minutes or until cooked. Remove from the oven and leave to cool.

To make the prawn sauce:

Melt the butter in a heavy-based saucepan, add the flour and cook for 1 minute, stirring constantly. Add the fish stock and white wine and stir until the sauce is smooth and thick. Add the sour cream, egg yolks, lemon juice and horseradish to heat through. Season with the salt and stir in the prawns.

To serve:

Turn out the terrine onto a serving platter. Garnish with the lemon slices and dill. Spoon some of the prawn sauce over the terrine and serve the remaining sauce separately.

500 g white fish, such as
   kingklip or kabeljou (kob)
250 ml milk
4 leeks, white part only,
   thinly sliced
50 g butter
50 ml cake flour
250 ml milk, extra
10 ml anchovy sauce or
   4 anchovy fillets, chopped
30 ml fresh lemon juice
1 x 220 g can salmon
3 jumbo eggs, separated
2.5 ml freshly ground
   black pepper
lemon slices and sprigs of
   fresh dill to garnish

Prawn sauce
50 g butter
50 ml cake flour
250 ml fish stock
75 ml dry white wine
125 ml sour cream
2 jumbo egg yolks
15 ml fresh lemon juice
5 ml horseradish sauce
2.5 ml salt
200 g prawns, cleaned, cooked
   and shelled

A terrine is the basis of many a lunch for those of you who have travelled in France.

The texture of a terrine is more coarse than that of a pâté and it is always baked.

Serve it sliced with crusty French or wholewheat bread.

Smoked Salmon Ramekins *with horseradish cream*

SERVES 6

To make the mousse:
Lightly coat six small ramekins or dariole moulds with cooking spray, or grease with butter or vegetable fat, and line each one with a slice of smoked salmon, leaving some of the salmon overlapping at the top of the ramekin. Beat together the cream cheese, yoghurt and horseradish sauce in a bowl until smooth. Mix in the cucumber or red pepper, chopped salmon and lemon juice. Sprinkle the gelatine over the cooled stock in a small heavy-based saucepan and heat, stirring until dissolved. Pour into the mousse mixture and stir until combined. Season with the salt and pepper only if necessary. Spoon the mousse mixture into the salmon-lined ramekins, neatly folding over the over-hanging salmon. Set in the refrigerator for a few hours or overnight.

To make the horseradish cream:
Combine the yoghurt, sour cream, horseradish sauce and dill. Season to taste with the salt and pepper.

To serve:
Invert the ramekins onto six plates. Spoon some sauce over each ramekin and garnish with lemon rind and a spoonful of caviar.

The clever cook can pass around crisp Melba toast or thinly sliced brown bread.

Mousse
6 large thin slices best quality smoked salmon or smoked salmon trout
100 ml plain cream cheese or cream cheese with chives
200 ml thick plain yoghurt
60 ml horseradish sauce
125 ml finely chopped, peeled and seeded cucumber or red pepper
125 ml finely chopped smoked salmon
30 ml fresh lemon juice
15 ml gelatine powder
125 ml cooled fish stock
salt and freshly ground black pepper
strips of lemon rind and caviar to garnish

Horseradish cream
125 ml thin natural yoghurt
125 ml sour cream
30 ml horseradish sauce or creamed horseradish
15 ml chopped fresh dill
salt and white pepper

Salmon is a superb delicacy. Choose salmon that has pale pink-gold flesh and is as fresh as possible. The best kind has fat striations present on the surface.

Baked Scottish Salmon *with dill hollandaise*

I serve the salmon on its own as a starter for a dinner party, or as a main course with the baked potatoes and the vegetable platter.

SERVES 4

To prepare the salmon:
Preheat the oven to 200 °C. Coat an ovenproof dish with cooking spray, or grease with butter or vegetable fat. Place the fish fillet skin side down in the dish and season with the oil, mustard, salt and pepper.

Bake for 20–30 minutes, depending on the thickness of the fillet. The flesh should still be slightly rare. After removing the fish from the oven, leave to rest for 5 minutes before portioning. Serve topped with fine green beans and dill hollandaise.

To make the dill hollandaise:
Fit the metal blade to the food processor. Add the egg yolks, lemon juice, mustard, dill and salt and process for 5 seconds to combine.

Heat the butter in the microwave at 100 per cent power until boiling point. With the food processor running, slowly pour the melted butter in a steady stream through the feed tube. Process for at least 60 seconds after adding the last of the butter.

The clever cook can refrigerate the leftover salmon and serve it cold with home-made mayonnaise and a fresh salad for a light lunch.

Baked potatoes
Use firm, smooth potatoes of a uniform size, without blemishes. New potatoes are unsuitable for baking. Scrub the potatoes and dry. Place on the oven-rack and bake at 180 °C for about 1 hour.

Test for readiness by squeezing the potato gently – it should feel soft to the touch. Cut a cross on top of each potato to allow steam to escape. Dot with butter or serve plain.

Seasonal vegetable platter
Combine a variety of seasonal vegetables, such as broccoli, baby carrots, baby beans and young marrows. Trim all the vegetables and steam very lightly. Arrange each group together on a large heated platter, and spoon over 100 ml melted butter combined with 30 ml fresh lemon juice. Season with salt and freshly ground black pepper.

1 side fresh Scottish or
  Norwegian salmon, skin on,
  bones removed
100 ml olive oil
30 ml good quality
  prepared French mustard
salt and freshly ground
  black pepper
100 g fine green beans,
  steamed

Dill hollandaise
3 jumbo egg yolks
30 ml fresh lemon juice
5 ml prepared mustard
2.5 ml chopped fresh dill
a pinch of salt
125 g butter, melted

courgette-stuffed *Chicken*

My girls love the taste of this chicken dish as the combination of the courgettes and honey glaze is absolutely delicious!

SERVES 4

Preheat the oven to 180 °C. Rinse the chicken quarters and pat dry with paper towelling. Heat the olive oil in a heavy-based saucepan and sauté the courgettes until glazed. Remove from the heat and add the bread and beaten egg and mix lightly. Season with the salt and pepper.

Loosen the skin on each chicken quarter to form a pocket. Spoon a quarter of the stuffing into each chicken piece. Place the chicken on the rack on an oven-roasting pan and baste with the honey. Bake for 50 minutes, basting every now and then, or until the chicken is tender and cooked through.

1 chicken, quartered (or 4 thigh and leg portions)
50 ml olive oil
6 courgettes (baby marrow), grated (do not peel)
3 slices fresh white bread, crusts removed, crumbled
1 jumbo egg, beaten
5 ml salt
2.5 ml freshly ground white pepper
200 ml honey

Rosh Hashanah or Thanksgiving *Turkey*

*A good turkey is compact, with a pearly-white skin and a broad plump breast.
I enjoy preparing a turkey for any festive occasion. If you are cooking a very
large turkey, make sure beforehand that your oven is large enough to hold it.*

SERVES 10

To prepare the turkey:
Preheat the oven to 180 °C.
Clean the turkey thoroughly.
Combine the salt, crushed
garlic, pepper, seasoning salt,
garlic salt, ginger and paprika,
and rub the mixture into the
skin as well as under the breast
skin and inside the cavity of the
turkey. Sprinkle the lemon juice
into the cavity and place the
onion inside. Place the turkey
in deep oven-roasting pan and
pour over the cooking oil. Roast
uncovered, basting occasionally
and taking care not to prick
the skin. Depending on the size
of the turkey, roast for about
3 hours or for 50 minutes per
500 g of the weight of the
turkey, adding an additional
20 minutes at the end of the
calculated roasting time. Turn
the turkey every 30 minutes.
Fifteen minutes prior to serving,
pour over the orange juice and
rind. Place the turkey on a bed
of rocket on a serving platter.

To make the gravy:
Pour off the juices from the
roasting pan into a small heavy-
based saucepan. Add the water,
stock cubes, flour and salt and
pepper. Cook until thickened.
    Spoon a little gravy over
the turkey to keep it moist and
serve the rest separately.

The clever cook can cover
the turkey with a sheet of
baking paper to prevent it from
becoming too dark during the
roasting process.

1 x whole turkey (note
    the weight)
10 ml salt
3 cloves garlic, crushed
5 ml freshly ground
    black pepper
2.5 ml seasoning salt
2.5 ml garlic salt
2.5 ml ground ginger
2.5 ml paprika
juice of 1 lemon
1 onion
250 ml cooking oil
juice and rind of 2 oranges
rocket to garnish

Gravy
250 ml water
2 chicken stock cubes
20 ml cake flour
salt and freshly ground
    black pepper

basic Roast Beef

It is most important to apply the correct cooking method to each meat cut. Grilling a slice of shin will result in a culinary disaster! Using scotch fillet for a stew on the other hand is extremely wasteful.

SERVES 6

To prepare the roast beef:
Preheat the oven to 180 °C. Season the meat with the salt, pepper, olive oil and garlic. Place the meat, fat side uppermost, on the rack of an oven-roasting pan. Oven-roast for:

Underdone or rare –
15 minutes per 500 g plus an extra 15 minutes; or an internal temperature of 60 °C if using a meat thermometer.

Medium (beef and lamb) –
20 minutes per 500 g plus an extra 20 minutes; or an internal temperature of 70 °C.

Well-done (lamb and veal) –
25 minutes per 500 g plus an extra 25 minutes; or an internal temperature of 80 °C. Well-done is not recommended for beef.

To make the basting:
Combine all the ingredients and baste the meat frequently during the roasting process.

Allow the meat to rest in the warming oven for 5–10 minutes before serving. This eases the task of carving, as the meat becomes slightly firmer.

To serve:
Carve slices of beef and serve with a baby potato salad.

The clever cook can also use prime rib, scotch fillet, fillet or rump. Well-ripened, top grade meat will produce the best results.

1.5–2 kg beef sirloin
10–15 ml salt
2.5 ml freshly ground
   black pepper
50 ml olive oil
2 cloves garlic, crushed

White wine basting
50 ml dry white wine
juice and rind of 1 lemon
50 ml cooking oil
2 cloves garlic, crushed
1 sprig each of fresh rosemary
   and thyme, chopped
2.5 ml salt
a pinch of freshly ground
   black pepper
5 ml grated lemon rind

Rack of Lamb *with green herb crust*

A rack of lamb traditionally consists of six to eight chops, but you can get just the size you want by specifying the number of chops. A rack is easy to carve – just cut down between the bones.

SERVES 4

To prepare the lamb:
Ask the butcher to chine the rack and saw through the backbone of the meat to facilitate carving. French the rib ends for 2.5 cm by carefully cutting through the connective tissue and removing the meat and fat from the rib ends. Season the meat with the olive oil, salt and pepper.

To make the herb crust:
Combine the breadcrumbs, olive oil, parsley and garlic. Spread the topping mixture onto the fat surface of the meat and refrigerate for 2 hours before roasting.

To cook the lamb:
Preheat the oven to 180 °C. Cover the rib ends with aluminium foil. Place the rack, topping side uppermost, on the rack of an oven-roasting pan and roast for:

Medium – 20–25 minutes per 500 g plus 20 minutes.

Well-done – 25–30 minutes per 500 g plus 25 minutes.

Allow the rack to rest for 10 minutes before cutting into chops and serving.

1 rack of lamb consisting of 8 chops, 15 cm in length
50 ml olive oil
5 ml salt
2.5 ml freshly ground black pepper

Green herb crust
250 ml fresh white breadcrumbs
50 ml olive oil
50 ml chopped fresh parsley
2 cloves garlic, crushed

the best ever *Chocolate Mousse*

SERVES 8

Break the chocolate into pieces and microwave 400 g at a time on 50 per cent power for 4 minutes or until melted. Allow the chocolate to cool to room temperature.

Using the same beaters throughout, firstly beat the egg whites until the soft peak stage and set aside. Lightly whip the cream and icing sugar until the cream holds its shape. Lastly, beat the egg yolks and the brandy.

Stir the melted chocolate into the egg yolks and mix until smooth. Using a metal spoon, fold in some of the beaten egg whites to lighten the texture of the chocolate mixture. Fold the chocolate mixture into the rest of the beaten egg whites. Finally fold in the cream.

Spoon into a serving bowl or into elegant glasses and refrigerate for a minimum of 2 hours. If preferred, decorate with chocolate curls and whipped cream.

The extravagant clever cook can use imported chocolate for an excellent end result. I do this for a limited number of guests and serve the mousse in crystal champagne flutes.

In the absence of a microwave, melt the chocolate in the top part of a double-boiler over boiling water.

800 g dark chocolate

7 eggs, separated

500 ml fresh cream

50 ml icing sugar

50 ml brandy or liqueur of choice

Mousse is the French name for foam or froth. It is a rich, airy mixture that depends on whisked egg white, whipped cream or both for its lightness and velvety texture. My nephew Michael says this mousse passes the test, as a spoon can stand upright when scooped into the chocolate.

espresso *Crème Brûlée*

For this coffee-flavoured dessert you need to use a set of ovenproof cups or dishes and, for best results, it must be prepared a day in advance. Chocolate-coated coffee beans add a chic finishing touch.

SERVES 8

Preheat the oven to 160 °C. Lightly grease eight ovenproof cups or small ramekins and stand them on a baking tray.

Heat the cream in a heavy-based saucepan until scalding point. Stir in the coffee and the liqueur. Beat the egg yolks until pale and creamy in a mixing bowl. Pour the hot mixture onto the egg yolks, whisking thoroughly. Stir in the castor sugar.

Pour the mixture into the ovenproof containers. Place the ramekins in a roasting pan lined with three sheets of newspaper. Pour in hot water to come halfway up the sides of the ramekins. Bake for about 45 minutes or until the custards are set. The custard should come away from the side of the cup but the centre should still be a bit wobbly. Remove from the oven and allow to cool. Chill the crème brûlées in the refrigerator overnight.

Prior to serving, sprinkle about 15 ml of brown sugar evenly over the top of each custard and caramelise using a blowtorch or place the ramekins under the grill of a very hot oven. Serve immediately. Decorate with a few regular or chocolate-coated coffee beans.

The clever cook who prefers a plain crème brûlée can prepare this recipe in exactly the same manner, omitting the coffee and liqueur and reducing the egg yolks to eight.

1 litre fresh cream
100 ml double-strength
  espresso
30 ml Kahlúa or Tia Maria
  liqueur
12 large egg yolks
150 g castor sugar
125 ml brown sugar to
  caramelize
regular or chocolate-coated
  coffee beans for decoration
  (optional)

Black and white with

geometric lines and square plates create a crisp yet

informal setting on the verandah. Set the stage with oriental

elements, origami fortunes wrapped in little black boxes and bound

with red velvet, Phalaenopsis orchids, rows of tiny tea lights and with

Chinese lanterns to offer soft light at sunset.

chilled Courgette and Cucumber Soup

SERVES 4

Heat the butter in a large heavy-based saucepan and sauté the leeks, potatoes, cucumber and courgettes until tender. Add the heated stock and bring to the boil. Simmer, covered, for about 20 minutes or until the vegetables are tender.

Purée the mixture in batches in a food processor fitted with a metal blade until smooth. Add the yoghurt. Season with the lemon juice, lemon rind, salt and pepper. Chill the soup and serve ice cold. Swirl with yoghurt and garnish with the chives prior to serving.

The clever cook can combine this soup with the Gazpacho (page 165). Spoon each soup into its own half of a soup plate (the consistency of these soups means they won't 'run' into each other) to create a complete colour and taste sensation.

50 g butter
8 leeks, white part only, thinly sliced
3 potatoes, peeled and cubed
1 English cucumber, skin on and cubed
1 kg courgettes (baby marrows), ends removed and sliced
1 litre hot vegetable stock
500 ml plain yoghurt plus extra for serving
30 ml fresh lemon juice
rind of 1 lemon
salt and freshly ground rainbow pepper
50 ml fresh chives

This recipe is based on the traditional vichyssoise, but incorporates the delicate flavour of cucumber and courgette, resulting in a lighter, more flavourful soup that is ideal for an alfresco meal.

chunky *Mushroom Soup*

This soup is my daughter Marissa's favourite. The different kinds of mushroom ensure a soup of an excellent and varied texture.

SERVES 6–8

Heat 50 g of the butter in a heavy-based saucepan and sauté the large mushrooms and the rosemary until the mushrooms are tender. Set aside and discard the rosemary.

Melt the rest of the butter in the same saucepan and stir in the flour until smooth. Stir in the heated stock and bring to the boil. Add the leeks and the rest of the mushrooms, excluding the open brown mushrooms. Add the soup, cream and sherry. Season with the salt and pepper.

Ladle the soup into bowls and place 1 large mushroom into each serving. Top with the spring onion and serve with crispy, warmed rolls.

150 g butter
6–8 large open brown mushrooms
1 sprig of fresh rosemary
125 ml cake flour
1 litre hot vegetable stock
3 leeks, white part only, sliced
500 g brown mushrooms, thickly sliced
300 g whole white button mushrooms
300 g white button mushrooms, sliced
1 x 400 g can cream of mushroom soup
250 ml fresh cream
30 ml medium or cream sherry
salt and freshly ground black pepper
50 ml chopped spring onions

phyllo *Fish Parcels*

SERVES 6

To make the filling:

Melt the butter in a heavy-based saucepan and sauté the onions. Add the mushrooms and cook until the liquid has evaporated. Add the fish and cook for 10–15 minutes or until the fish is done.

Combine the cornflour and the milk to form a paste, then add it to the fish mixture together with the cream and cheese. Cook over low heat until thickened. Season to taste with the lemon juice, salt and pepper. Set the mixture aside.

To make the phyllo parcels:

Preheat the oven to 180 °C. Brush two sheets of the pastry with the melted butter followed by a sprinkling of breadcrumbs. Place on top of each other on a board. Butter a third sheet and place over the other two at an angle.

Place a large spoonful of the fish mixture in the centre. Bring the corners of the phyllo together and tie loosely with string. Separate and tear the edges to form a jagged frill. Brush with the melted butter. Repeat until you have six parcels. Place the parcels on a greased and floured baking tray. Bake for 25 minutes.

To serve:

Remove the string and re-tie the phyllo parcels with a spring onion or a chive.

The clever cook can add a dash of cayenne pepper to the fish mixture if desired.

I often prepare the parcels in advance and refrigerate them overnight on the prepared baking tray. Remember to keep the phyllo pastry covered with a damp cloth while preparing the parcels. This will prevent the phyllo from drying out.

125 g butter
2 onions, chopped
500 g white button mushrooms, sliced
1 kg kabeljou (kob) or kingklip, filleted and cut into strips
60 ml cornflour
30 ml milk
125 ml fresh cream
250 ml grated cheddar cheese
30 ml fresh lemon juice
salt and freshly ground black pepper
500 g phyllo pastry
extra 125 g butter, melted
50 g dried breadcrumbs
fresh chives or long, thin strips of spring onion

Phyllo is a very light, thin and delicate pastry widely used in the cookery of the Middle East. Phyllo is available either fresh or frozen from supermarkets, delicatessens and Greek restaurants. Despite its delicate texture, phyllo is one of the easiest of all pastries to use.

Tuna Steak
with wasabi mayonnaise

I use ready-sliced tuna steaks and ensure that they are neatly trimmed and of even thickness. Make sure that the fish is at room temperature before cooking. Most people enjoy fresh tuna rare, but my family prefer it cooked medium to well-done.

SERVES 4

100 ml olive oil
10 ml honey
20 ml soy sauce
100 ml coarsely ground
  black pepper
4 tuna steaks, 1 cm thick
fresh coriander and lime wedges
  to garnish

Wasabi mayonnaise
300 ml cooking oil
50 g chopped fresh
  coriander leaves
2 jumbo egg yolks
20 ml fresh lemon juice
10 ml wasabi paste
a pinch of salt

To prepare the tuna steaks:
Combine the olive oil, honey, soy sauce and pepper together in a bowl. Dip each tuna steak into the oil mixture, coating evenly. Heat a large, non-stick griddle pan until hot. Fry the tuna steaks for 3–4 minutes on each side or until the required degree of doneness. (The tuna steaks can also be baked in a casserole dish at 180 °C for 30 minutes or until cooked.)
  Serve immediately garnished with coriander and with lime wedges and wasabi mayo.

To make the mayonnaise:
Combine the oil and coriander leaves together in a small bowl and set aside. Whisk the egg yolks with the lemon juice, wasabi paste and salt in a food processor fitted with a plastic blade until thick. Add the oil mixture, a few drops at a time, while processing. As the mixture begins to thicken, add the oil in a thin, steady stream.

Cumin-roasted Spatchcock Chicken
with coriander and apple glaze

SERVES 4

Preheat the oven to 200 °C. Rub the chicken quarters with the olive oil and toss in the cumin and the salt. Heat a heavy-based non-stick frying pan and brown the quartered chickens over high heat. Transfer to a roasting pan and set aside.

Using the same frying pan, bring the onion, apple juice, brown sugar, cider vinegar, tomato sauce and orange rind to the boil, stirring to incorporate the sediment from he pan. Boil until thickened and syrupy. Coat the chicken with the apple glaze. Roast for 25–30 minutes or until tender and cooked. Garnish with the sprigs of fresh coriander.

1 spatchcock chicken, quartered
60 ml olive oil
15 ml ground cumin
10 ml salt
2 onions, chopped
250 ml apple juice
50 ml brown sugar
15 ml cider vinegar
30 ml tomato sauce
grated rind of 1 orange
a few sprigs of fresh coriander

A spatchcock chicken is prepared by cutting along either side of the backbone of the chicken and removing the backbone. Once the backbone is removed press down on the breastbone to flatten the bird.

no-roast Roast Beef

I always prepare this recipe when I am hosting a large crowd and am unsure of the punctuality of some of the guests.

SERVES 6

To prepare the roast beef:
Prepare the beef at least 2 hours before you intend roasting it by removing the joint from the refrigerator and allowing the meat to come to room temperature. Preheat the oven to 250 °C.

Rub the meat with the salt and pepper and spread with the olive oil and garlic. Place the meat on the rack of an oven-roasting pan and place it in the oven. Roast for 5 minutes per 500 g. Without opening the oven door, switch off the heat and leave for a further 2 hours. DO NOT, under any circumstances, open the oven door during this time.

When the 2 hours are up, open the door and, without removing the roasting pan from the oven, touch the beef with your finger. If it feels hot, go ahead and serve it. However, as some ovens do not retain their heat as well as others, you may find the beef on the lukewarm side. If so, close the door, switch the oven back to 250 °C and give it a further 10–15 minutes. This will raise the internal temperature of the beef without affecting its rareness.

Serve accompanied by gravy made with the pan juices. Thicken with a little cornflour or gravy powder mixed to a paste with a little cold water. Or serve this delicious mustard sauce on the side.

Mustard sauce
Combine a jar of good quality mustard of your choice and an equal quantity of fresh cream. Heat, but do not boil. Your guests will all want this recipe and have visions of you having spent endless hours over a simmering double boiler!

1 x 2.5 kg deboned and
    rolled beef joint (or joint of
    2 or 3 ribs of beef)
salt and freshly ground
    black pepper
50 ml olive oil
2 cloves garlic, crushed
watercress to garnish

mouthwatering Slow-cooked Oxtail

SERVES 8

Preheat the oven to 160 °C. Brown the oxtail pieces in the heated cooking oil in a large heavy-based casserole dish with a lid. Add the onion and sauté. Add the salt, pepper, bay leaves, garlic, stock, wine and tomatoes and cover with the lid.

Place the casserole in the oven for 3 hours, or until the meat is tender. Add the celery and carrots and return to the oven for another 30 minutes. Remove the bay leaves and add the frozen peas 15 minutes before serving, sprinkled with the parsley. Top with watercress and serve with rice and a salad.

The clever cook can substitute 4.5 kg sliced neck of lamb for the oxtail pieces.

3 oxtails, cut into joints
30 ml cooking oil
2 onions, sliced
10 ml salt
2.5 ml freshly ground
   black pepper
2 bay leaves
2 cloves garlic, crushed
1 litre hot beef stock
250 ml dry white wine
1 x 410 g can whole peeled
   tomatoes, quartered
250 g celery stalks, sliced
400 g peeled baby carrots
500 ml frozen peas
watercress to garnish

Oxtail is one of the most comforting winter dishes. The flavour is

rich, and the long, slow cooking develops the soft, gelatinous texture.

Oxtail is best cooked the day before serving and refrigerated

overnight. The fat will solidify on the surface, making it easy

to remove before the dish is reheated.

Salad of Roasted Baby Beets
with balsamic vinegar dressing

SERVES 4

Preheat the oven to 180 °C. Wash the baby beetroot and trim the tops, leaving on a little of the leafy stalks and roots. Pat the beetroot dry.

Cover a baking tray with a sheet of aluminium foil and spread the rock salt in the centre. Nestle the beetroot in the rock salt and scatter with the thyme, tearing the stems into smaller sprigs. Scrunch the foil and bring the edges together to enclose the beetroot and seal. Bake for 15–20 minutes or until the baby beets are tender, then set aside to cool slightly. Wearing a pair of disposable gloves (to avoid staining your hands), use a thin-bladed knife to peel the beetroot while they are still warm. Cut each beetroot in half vertically.

Heat the butter in a heavy-based frying pan. When the butter starts to foam, toss in the beetroot and cook, turning frequently, until the beetroot are coated and glossy in appearance. Add the balsamic vinegar and garlic and bubble until the liquid is reduced and syrupy.

Serve warm, garnished with fresh bay leaves, or at room temperature with cold roast beef.

The clever cook can buy the smallest fresh beetroot available. If baby beetroot are unavailable, increase the baking time accordingly. After peeling, cut the beetroot into 1 cm thick slices before glazing in the butter and balsamic vinegar.

As an alternative, combine the cooked beetroot with quartered toasted red onion, red baby spinach leaves, coriander and crumbed goat's cheese. Drizzle with olive oil and sprinkle with freshly ground black pepper (see photograph below).

500 g baby beetroot
200 g rock salt
2–3 sprigs fresh thyme
50 g butter
100 ml balsamic vinegar
4 cloves garlic, crushed
fresh bay leaves to garnish

To avoid losing any of the rich red colour, the beetroot should not be peeled or cut before cooking. When buying fresh beetroot, look for those that are smooth and firm to the touch with a good, round shape.

Mushroom *trio*

300 g wild or portabello
  mushrooms, sliced
300 g shiitake mushrooms,
  sliced
200 g oyster mushrooms, sliced
100 ml olive oil
50 g unsalted butter
15 ml chopped fresh thyme
salt and freshly ground
  black pepper
250 ml fresh cream
30 ml snipped fresh chives
200 g parmesan cheese
  shavings

Sauté all the mushrooms in the heated olive oil in a heavy-based frying pan until golden brown and completely tender. Add the butter and thyme to the frying pan and season to taste with the salt and pepper. Once the butter starts to melt, stir in the cream and chives. Cook for another 2–3 minutes or until reduced.

Transfer the mushroom mixture onto individual serving plates and scatter the parmesan shavings on top. Serve with some crusty bread.

The clever cook can use a combination of sliced brown and white mushrooms for a tasty alternative.

Mushrooms are remarkable in their ability to complement both robust and delicate flavours and their attractive shape can add much to the appearance of a dish.

Spicy Mashed Potatoes *with onions and pine nuts*

SERVES 6

To make the mashed potatoes:
Cook the potatoes in boiling salted water in a large heavy-based saucepan until tender. Drain the potatoes, return to the saucepan and keep off the heat. Add the butter, some of the milk and salt and pepper to taste. Crush with a potato masher. Beat the potatoes with a fork until they are light and fluffy, adding more milk and salt and pepper as required.

To make the onions:
Heat the oil in a non-stick frying pan and fry the onions over medium to high heat, tossing frequently until they are cooked and some of the onion is crisp and golden. Add the salt and pepper to taste.

To serve:
Serve the potatoes covered with the onions and the oil in which the onions were cooked. Sprinkle with the toasted pine nuts and top with a grinding of black pepper.

3 red onions, peeled and
   finely sliced
50 ml olive oil
salt and freshly ground
   black pepper
100 ml toasted pine nuts

Mashed potatoes
1 kg potatoes, peeled and
   halved
200 g butter
100 ml hot milk
salt and freshly ground
   black pepper

Choose floury potatoes if possible. When cooked sufficiently, the potatoes should break under pressure of a fork but not be mushy. Overcooking or cutting potatoes into small pieces makes them waterlogged and they lose flavour. Always add hot milk for fluffy potatoes as cold milk makes the potatoes sticky.

custard-coated *Mini Malva Puddings*

I 'copied' this idea from Stan and Pete, the renowned kosher caterers in Johannesburg. Hats off to Stan, Dennis, Ido, Jeff and the team for serving our community so elegantly at numerous Simchas!

SERVES 12

To make the puddings:
Preheat the oven to 180 °C. Beat the sugar and the eggs in a food processor using the plastic blade. Beat in the apricot jam.

Sift the flour, bicarbonate of soda and salt into a separate bowl. Melt the butter in a small heavy-based saucepan and add the vinegar and the milk.

Fold the dry ingredients and the milk mixture alternately into the egg mixture. Pour the batter into individual greased ramekins up to two-thirds full and bake in the oven for 20 minutes or until cooked. Loosen the edges of the puddings with a palette knife.

To make the malva sauce:
Combine all the sauce ingredients in a small heavy-based saucepan and bring to the boil. Spoon the sauce over the puddings as soon as they come out of the oven. Pierce the puddings a few times to allow the sauce to soak in.

To make the custard sauce:
Heat the milk in a heavy-based saucepan until warm. Remove the saucepan from the stove.

Whisk the egg yolks and sugar together until creamy and pour into the milk, whisking constantly. Stir the sauce over low heat until it coats the back of a wooden spoon. Do not boil the sauce as it will curdle.

Stir in the orange juice and rind. Remove the sauce from the stove and set aside to cool. When cold stir in the cream.

To serve:
Invert the ramekins onto serving plates and coat with a thin layer of the custard sauce, serving the remainder of the custard on the side. Serve hot.

The clever cook can use orange juice or cognac instead of the sherry for the sauce. Piercing the puddings with a fork will aid the absorption of the sauce.

500 ml castor sugar
4 jumbo eggs
30 ml smooth apricot jam
500 ml cake flour
10 ml bicarbonate of soda
2.5 ml salt
60 ml butter
10 ml white vinegar
250 ml milk

Malva sauce
250 ml fresh cream
125 g butter
125 ml white sugar
125 ml medium cream sherry

Custard sauce
500 ml milk
6 jumbo egg yolks
125 g white sugar
juice and grated rind
   of 1 orange
100 ml whipped cream

flop-proof Meringues

As the title of this recipe suggests, these meringues are a winner every time. My family enjoys them slightly under-baked and chewy!

MAKES 24

Preheat the oven to 100 °C. Using an electric beater, beat the egg whites and salt until soft peaks start to form. Gradually add the castor sugar and icing sugar, beating after each addition. Add the lemon juice and beat for a couple of seconds. Spoon or pipe the meringue onto a baking tray lined with baking paper.

Bake at 100 °C for 1 hour, then at 50 °C for another hour. Switch off the oven and leave the meringues, with the door closed, for 2–4 hours.

The clever cook can double this mixture and store the meringues in an airtight container for 3–4 weeks.

5 jumbo egg whites
5 ml salt
150 g castor sugar
150 g sifted icing sugar
10 ml fresh lemon juice

peach and cherry *Trifles*

SERVES 6

To make the trifles:

Bring the cream, milk, sugar and vanilla essence to the boil in a heavy-based saucepan. Beat the egg yolks in a large bowl and pour the hot mixture onto the egg yolks, beating constantly. Return the mixture to the saucepan and cook over a low heat, stirring constantly until the custard is thick enough to coat the back of a wooden spoon. Cover and set aside to cool.

To assemble:

Place the crushed biscuits at the base of six serving glasses and sprinkle with the framboise liqueur or sherry. Layer the peach slices and cherries on top of the crushed biscuit. Chill for 30 minutes. Top with the custard mixture. If desired, top with a dollop of whipped cream dusted with icing sugar.

300 ml fresh cream

100 ml milk

50 g castor sugar

5 ml vanilla essence

6 jumbo egg yolks

200 g amaretti biscuits, crushed

120 ml crème de framboise liqueur or cream sherry

2 ripe peaches, peeled and sliced, or the canned equivalent, drained and sliced

150 g stoned cherries, or the canned equivalent, drained

Trifle, the great English dessert, traditionally contains sponge cake soaked in alcohol.

This delicious variation uses crushed almond biscuits, but still incorporates the flavour

of a raspberry liqueur or a good, sweet sherry.

Strawberries *with hibiscus and basil syrup*

SERVES 8

Heat the sugar and water in a heavy-based saucepan, stirring occasionally. Add the lemon rind. Bring the syrup to the boil and boil for about 5 minutes. Remove the rind. Bring the syrup to the boil again and stir in the lemon juice, tea bags and basil leaves.

Remove the saucepan from the heat and leave the tea bags to infuse for 20 minutes. Strain the syrup and set aside to cool.

Place the strawberries in a bowl, add the syrup and stir gently. Refrigerate until ready to serve decorated with small basil leaves.

The clever cook can use fresh mango instead of the strawberries. The remaining syrup keeps successfully in a sealed jar in the refrigerator for up to three weeks.

500 g granulated or
    castor sugar
1 litre water
grated rind of 1 lemon
30 ml fresh lemon juice
4 rosehip and hibiscus tea bags
4 fresh basil leaves
1 kg fresh strawberries,
    washed and hulled
small fresh basil leaves
    for decoration

My family loves this dessert and often plunge dried mango into the leftover syrup. I usually

serve it in individual bowls with a scoop of yoghurt ice cream (page 217).

Yoghurt Ice Cream
with burnt honey and cashew nut topping

SERVES 8

To make the ice cream:
Combine the egg yolks, condensed milk and castor sugar in the bowl of an electric mixer and beat until light and fluffy. Add the vanilla essence.

Whip the cream in a separate bowl until it begins to hold its shape. Fold the cream into the egg mixture and beat until combined. Stir in the yoghurt and beat until mixed through. Beat the egg whites until stiff and fold in using a metal spoon. Pour the mixture into a non-stick loaf pan or a mould coated with cooking spray and freeze.

To make the topping:
Heat the honey in a heavy-based frying pan until it begins to caramelize and soften. Pour the honey onto a sheet of greaseproof paper and sprinkle the cashew nuts on top and cool. Once set, break the caramelized honey into shards and use to decorate the top of the ice cream.

The clever cook can place the praline in the freezer to speed up the setting process.

6 jumbo eggs, separated
1 x 225 g can condensed milk
250 ml castor sugar
5 ml vanilla essence
500 ml fresh cream
500 ml full-cream natural
    yoghurt

Topping
250 ml honey
150 g chopped, unsalted
    cashew nuts

This is my perfected recipe – the yoghurt takes away the sharp sweet taste of the condensed

milk, but the ice cream is still sweet enough to satisfy the average 'sweet tooth'!

Shereen's favourite *Butterscotch Sauce*

Shereen Fihrer loves this sauce and always serves it for a special occasion.
It is decadently rich but oh so yummy!

MAKES 500 ML

250 ml thick fresh cream
100 g butter, cut into cubes
250 ml brown sugar
250 ml white sugar
2.5 ml salt
250 ml golden syrup
5 ml vanilla essence

Place all the ingredients, except the vanilla essence, in a heavy-based saucepan. Cook over low heat, stirring constantly with a wooden spoon until the butter is completely melted and the sugars are dissolved. Increase the heat to medium and bring the mixture to a gentle boil. Boil without stirring for 5 minutes. Remove the saucepan from the heat and allow to cool for 20 minutes, whisking occasionally. Whisk in the vanilla essence. Serve the sauce warm with Yoghurt Ice Cream (page 217).

chilled *Red Berry Sauce*

Raspberries can be the most elusive of summer fruits. They arrive with the first of the summer fruits, then disappear during the hottest months to return at the start of autumn.

MAKES 500 ML

Process the raspberries and water in the bowl of a food processor fitted with the metal blade. Combine the raspberry purée, jelly powder and sugar in a heavy-based saucepan and cook over medium-low heat, stirring continuously with a wooden spoon until the jelly and the sugar has dissolved. Bring to the boil and boil for 1 minute without stirring. Remove the saucepan from the heat and stir in the lemon juice. Allow to cool. Stir in the liqueur and the strawberries. Refrigerate for at least 1 hour. Serve the sauce chilled with Yoghurt Ice Cream (page 217).

2 x 125 g punnets fresh raspberries

50 ml water

100 ml red currant jelly powder

100 ml white sugar

15 ml fresh lemon juice

15ml Cointreau or orange-flavoured liqueur

1 x 250 g punnet fresh strawberries, hulled and chopped

Glossary

Baking: Cooking in the oven by means of dry heat. This method is used for cakes, biscuits, pastries and many other dishes.

Baking blind: Baking pastry cases without a filling. To blind bake, first line the pastry dish with pastry and trim the edges. Cover with greaseproof paper and weigh down with dried beans. Bake at 200 °C for 15 minutes, then remove the greaseproof paper and beans and return to the oven for a few minutes to dry out.

Basting: To spoon the pan juices over meat or poultry during roasting, thus preventing it from drying out.

Beating: To vigorously mix, using a spoon or a beater. An upward circular movement should be used to incorporate air into the mixture.

Blanching: To immerse fruit or vegetables briefly in boiling water. The cooking process is stopped by immersing the fruit or vegetable into ice water.

Blending: Mixing cornflour or flour to a paste with cold milk, water or stock before adding boiling liquid. Used for preparing soups, stews or gravies.

Boiling: Cooking in liquid at a temperature of 100 °C (at sea level). Vegetables, rice, pasta and syrups that need to be reduced are usually boiled. Meat, fish and poultry must be simmered as boiling causes shrinkage and loss of flavour.

Browning: Meat that is to be pot-roasted, stewed or casseroled should first be browned in hot oil or a dry heavy-based pan to seal it and prevent the loss of juices that give flavour to the meat.

Casserole: A heatproof, moderately deep baking dish with a tightly fitting lid, used for cooking meat, poultry or vegetables. The food is usually served directly from the dish.

Chopping: Cutting food into small pieces. The ingredients are placed on a chopping board and a sharp knife is used with a quick up-and-down action. Food processors may also be used for chopping.

Creaming: Butter (or margarine) and sugar beaten together until pale yellow in colour and with a light, fluffy texture. This method is used for cakes and puddings containing a high percentage of shortening.

Croutons: Small cubes of fried or toasted bread that are usually served as an accompaniment or garnish to soup.

Dough: A thick mixture of uncooked flour and liquid, often combined with other ingredients and used for making bread, pastry, scones or biscuits.
Flaking: Breaking up cooked fish into coarse flakes by using a fork.

Folding in: Combining a whisked or creamed mixture with other ingredients so that it retains lightness. It is used for certain cake mixtures and for meringues and soufflés. A typical example is folding dry flour into a beaten egg and sugar mixture for a sponge cake. Important points to remember are that the mixture must be folded very lightly and that it must not be agitated more than is absolutely necessary because, with every movement, some of the air bubbles are broken down. Do not use an electric beater.

Frying: The process of cooking food in hot fat or cooking oil. Most food should be coated before frying. There are two main methods:

Deep-frying To cook food in sufficient fat or cooking oil to cover it completely. This method is used for batter-coated fish, chipped potatoes, doughnuts and fritters.
Shallow frying: To cook food such as escalopes or schnitzels, chops, small sausages or fish in a little fat or oil in a frying pan. Fish cakes require slightly deeper oil.

A deep pan with a wire basket is required, as well as sufficient oil to fill two-thirds of the pan. The oil must be pure and free from moisture, to avoid spluttering or boiling over, and it must be heated to the correct temperature or the food will be either soggy and grease-sodden or overcooked and burnt.

To test that the oil is at the correct temperature, place a 25 mm cube of white bread in the cooking oil. If it turns golden-brown in 60 seconds, the oil is ready for cooking raw food. For cooked foods, the cube of bread should change to a golden-brown colour within 40 seconds.

Garnish: An edible decoration, such as parsley, watercress, wild rocket or lemon slices or wedges arranged around or on top of a savoury dish to improve its appearance and flavour.

Glaze: For example, beaten egg, egg white or milk that is painted over certain sweets or savouries, such as pies, to give them a glossy surface.

A meat glaze suitable for savouries can be made from home-made meat stock reduced substantially by rapid boiling.

Syrup or jam is used to glaze fruit tarts.

Grate: To reduce foods, such as firm cheese or vegetables, to small shreds by rubbing against a rough or sharp perforated surface.

Grilling: Cooking food by direct heat under a grill or over a hot fire. Good quality, tender meat such as steak or chops, whole fish, including salmon, and fish cutlets are the foods most often cooked in this way.

Hollandaise: A rich sauce made with vinegar, butter and egg yolks and generally served with vegetables or fish. Herbs can be added to vary the flavour.

Infusing: Extracting flavour from spices, herbs, and so on, by steeping in boiling liquid. The resulting liquid is known as an infusion.

Kneading: To work dough with a pressing motion accompanied by folding and stretching. In bread-making, the knuckles are used; in pastry-making, the fingertips are used. In both cases, the outside of the dough is drawn into the centre.

Marinade: A seasoned mixture of oil and vinegar, lemon juice or wine in which food is left to soak over a given time. The marinade helps to soften the fibres of meat and fish and adds flavour to the food.

Piping: Applying whipped cream, icing or butter through a forcing bag and nozzle to decorate cakes, desserts, and so on. Also used for fluffy mashed potatoes and meringue. The bag may be made of cotton, nylon or plastic.

Purée: Fruit, vegetables, meat or fish which has been pounded, sieved or liquidized in an electric blender (usually after cooking) to give a smooth pulp.

Rind: The thin rind of an orange, lemon or lime, containing oil that gives a characteristic citrus flavour. Grate it using a fine grater, taking care not to remove any pith (the white part).

Roasting: In its true form, roasting means cooking by direct heat in front of an open fire. In other words, rotisserie cooking is true roasting.

However, the modern method is to place meat or poultry in the oven on the rack of an oven-roasting pan without any additional fat or cooking oil and to leave the pan uncovered. Only tender, top grade, ripened meat is suitable.

Rubbing in: A method of incorporating butter with flour when making shortcrust pastry, plain cakes or biscuits. Cut the butter into small pieces, add to the flour and, using only your fingertips, rub it in to give a crumbly rather than a smooth texture.

Sautéing: To cook in an open pan over a moderately high heat using butter or cooking oil. This method is usually used for softening vegetables such as onions, peppers or celery. The pan should be shaken so that the ingredients don't stick to the pan. A wide, shallow, heavy-based pan should be used.

Searing: Rapidly browning meat in a little fat before grilling or roasting.

Shredding: Slicing a food such as raw vegetables very finely. A sharp knife or coarse grater is generally used.

Simmering: Keeping a liquid just below boiling point (approximately 96 °C at sea level). First bring the liquid to the boil, then adjust the heat so that the surface of the liquid is kept just simmering.

Stock: The liquid produced when meat, bones, poultry, fish or vegetables are simmered with herbs and flavourings in water for several hours to extract their flavour. Stock forms the foundation of soups, sauces and stews and many savoury dishes.

Thickening: Giving body to soups, sauces or gravies by adding flour or cornflour (see also Blending).

Whipping or whisking: To beat air rapidly into a mixture using an egg beater, whisk or electric beater.

Conversion Charts

Metric	US cups	Imperial
5 ml	1 tsp	³⁄₁₆ fl oz
15 ml	1 Tbsp	½ fl oz
60 ml	4 Tbsp (¼ cup)	2 fl oz
80 ml	⅓ cup	2¾ fl oz
125 ml	½ cup	4½ fl oz
160 ml	⅔ cup	5½ fl oz
200 ml	¾ cup	7 fl oz
250 ml	1 cup	9 fl oz
100 g	–	3½ oz
250 g	–	9 oz
500 g	–	1 lb
750 g	–	1¾ lb
1 kg	–	2¼ lb

Oven temperatures

Celsius (°C)	Fahrenheit (°F)	Gas mark
100 °C	200 °F	¼
110 °C	225 °F	¼
120 °C	250 °F	½
140 °C	275 °F	1
150 °C	300 °F	2
160 °C	325 °F	3
180 °C	350 °F	4
190 °C	375 °F	5
200 °C	400 °F	6
220 °C	425 °F	7
230 °C	450 °F	8
240 °C	475 °F	9

Acknowledgements

My thanks to the best team effort in the world: Linda de Villiers (publishing manager) for your professionalism and encouragement in developing the exciting content. Joy Clack (editor) for being a perfectionist par excellence and for enjoying crossing every 't' and dotting every 'i'. Petal Palmer (designer) for your infectious enthusiasm, professional polish and brilliant design.

To Neil Corder (photographer), a true gentleman and perfectionist, Justine Kiggen (food stylist), a gentle professional and Tina Bester (décor stylist), who waved her technicolour magic wand – thank you for the fun we had in putting this book together.
Fay Lewis

The author and publishers also wish to thank the following persons and companies for their kind assistance and loan of props for photography:

Shereen Fihrer of Head Interiors; Gideon du Plessis and Wally Clack of Gideon's Flowers and Functions; Lauren Abelheim of Apsley House; Abe Opperman and Ben Theron of Hoy P'Loy; Susan McCoubrey of Loft Living; and the Directors and Management of Lejwe La Metsi Game Farm, Warmbaths.

Index of Recipes

Page numbers in *italic* type refer to photographs.